photos
for the future
2

SUTTON PUBLISHING

THE HISTORY CHANNEL.

First published in the United Kingdom in 2000 by
Sutton Publishing Limited · Phoenix Mill
Thrupp · Stroud · Gloucestershire · GL5 2BU

British Library Cataloguing in Publication Data
A catalogue record for this book is available from the British Library.

ISBN 0-7509-2703-8

Title page photograph: This photo was taken over fifty-two years ago and is of my father, auntie and grandmother on Christmas Day. This photo is important to me because owing to the effects of global warming I have not experienced a white Christmas (not one that I can remember). Even though my father was only young, he had many more to come. (Serena Fuller, Ashford School, **Secondary School Winner**)

Typeset in 11/14pt Gill Sans.
Typesetting and origination by
Sutton Publishing Limited.
Printed and bound in England by
J.H. Haynes & Co. Ltd, Sparkford.

Contents

Introduction

This book is the second selection of photographs which comes from a project begun two years ago by The History Channel to create a record of ordinary life in the twentieth century for future generations – hence its title, *Photos for the Future 2*. It is a unique collection, a collection never before published because it comes from ordinary people who sent us their photos.

When we started this project we had little idea that it would become such a success. To date the project has received over 12,000 photographs. What you see in this book represents only a small percentage of those photographs.

These photographs are history in two ways. In one sense this is a history of photography – not the photography of beautiful images by famous photographers, of national events and well-known people. This is an entirely different history because it's the history of photography by ordinary people recording generally commonplace events from their own lives.

Above all these photographs form a cultural history of Britain because they capture the shared experiences that have touched many of us in the twentieth century: the upheaval of two world wars, a family member's call to arms and the efforts on the home front, the economic hardships and the prosperity which brought to an expanding middle class things such as a first family car or a holiday abroad, and of course a first camera.

The captions for the photographs were written by their owners. They contain some wonderful stories and often express a very real awareness of their owner's own place as a participant in history.

We'd like to thank all of the people who sent us their photos, who went back to their own personal archives in the family photo album or who took a picture which they felt was of historical value. Without their participation the project would not have been possible.

We would also like to acknowledge the contributions of two organisations – English Heritage and the Royal British Legion. Their help in spreading the word and encouraging people to participate was invaluable.

We hope that this collection will become an historical reference for future generations. Above all we believe that it has encouraged people to explore their own family roots and we hope that in so doing they have discovered a bit more about themselves and where they come from.

Geoff Metzger
The History Channel

Acknowledgements

The History Channel would like to thank all the organisations and individuals who cooperated with us on the project to make it such a success: English Heritage for helping to promote the initiative and for hosting exhibitions at the following properties: Bayham Old Abbey (Kent), Belsay Hall & Gardens (Northumberland), Kenilworth Castle (Warwickshire), Kirby Hall (Northamptonshire) and the National Monuments Record (Swindon).

The many museums and galleries hosting exhibitions, including Bourne Hall Museum & Library (Surrey), City of Westminster Archives Centre, Coalbrookdale Museum of Iron (Shropshire), Dover Museum, Letchworth Museum & Art Gallery, Museum of Oxford, Museum of Science and Industry (Manchester), Plas Mawr – Cadw (Conwy), Royal Norfolk Regimental Museum – Norfolk Museums Service, The People's Palace (Glasgow), The Royal Armouries (Leeds), The Potteries Museum & Art Gallery (Stoke-on-Trent), West Berkshire Heritage Service, Whitby Archives & Heritage Centre, Wigan Pier and Y Tabernacl – The Museum of Modern Art (Powys).

Our panel of judges – Professor Bill Speck from the Historical Association, Mike Corbishley from English Heritage, Toby Waller from Sutton Publishing, Andrew Dean from The Royal British Legion, Julie Ann Quiery and Mark Lynch from Hulton Getty Picture Collection, Geoff Metzger from The History Channel.

The Royal British Legion for publicising the project to their members.

The Campaign for Museums for hosting a virtual exhibition on their 24 Hour Museum website.

The Historical Association, LEAs and County Councils for helping to communicate the initiative.

And finally we would like to thank all the companies and individuals who worked so hard to make the project happen – Nicki Harris, Anna Brady, Kulvinder Sahota, Michelle Reed, Charlotte Nell, Jo Mitchell, Mike Simpkins, Centurion Press, e-crmdata.com, Imagecare.com, Euroworld Direct Marketing, Graphix Imaging and the team of project co-ordinators – Max Kredal, Ciara Hardman, Jinal Patel, James Buchanan, Samantha Szepel-Lukowska and Sara Griffiths.

childhood

Ghost train. During the 1950s and '60s it was frequently the practice of schools to take children on a day trip, often educational. I went with groups from Stoke to Rhyl, Llandudno, Morecambe Bay, the Lake District, Regents Park Zoo, Chester Zoo, and so on. If there was a fairground or pleasure beach it was irresistible. Here two girls from the Priory Junior School, Trentham, Staffordshire, enjoy being scared out of their wits. (Donald Morris, **Overall Winner**)

This is a photograph of my grandchildren, Amy and her two brothers, James and baby Gareth. They were born and live in the London area, where their roots are, with my son Martyn, their Welsh father, and Melanie, their English mother. In the year 2000 at the start of a new millennium I see in their eyes a look of fun and adventure which gives me confidence in the future. It is the same look that I saw in my great-grandmother's eyes all those years ago. (Arthur Colburn)

Ralph died not long after this photograph was taken, from the kind of illness that can be treated nowadays. His brother Edward had died before that. My great-aunt Flo lost her mind from the shock of losing both her children. Death in childhood was common in that period, but still just as terrible. (Dudley George)

My father and his older brother Ron were the Pear's Soap babies of 1924. The photos were displayed in chemists around the country and in their local chemists for many years. My father is now seventy-nine and his brother Ron is eighty. (Geoffrey Hill)

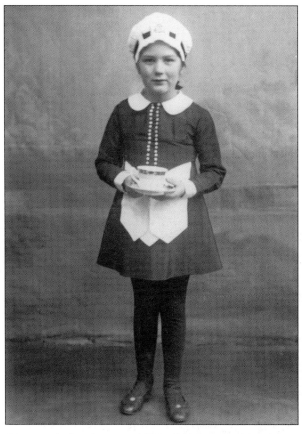

My grandfather and me in 1979. My grandfather sadly died in 1981. It's personal to me because this is one of very few photos I had with him. It was taken in India, in a studio, when I was three years old. Its interest to future generations is the relationship between very old generations and very young generations. The historical value is of the grandfather and the grandchild to be remembered together for the future. (Dalbir Lally)

My treat in London as a 1930s child was to visit a Lyons Corner House where nice waitresses or 'Nippies' served our afternoon tea with speed and efficiency to genteel background music played by a small orchestra. At a fancy dress party, I was upset to find that my 'Nippy' outfit, lent by Lyons, seemed in stark contrast to the prettier costumes of my friends, so I was surprised to win first prize! Too young at six to understand the advertising value of my success to J. Lyons & Co., I enjoyed the 2 lb box of chocolates they sent as a reward! (Jane Crabbe)

My children Sam and Amy watching the solar eclipse on 11 August 1999. As a historical event it has obvious significance, but it has extra poignancy to me as they will never be three and five and so full of wonder again, nor will we share another eclipse together. (Michael Copsey)

My father aged ten with his first bicycle. He was the first in the family to attend a grammar school; first King Edward's Grammar School, Five Ways, Birmingham, and later King Edward's School, New Street, Birmingham, where his name is on the roll of honour opposite that of J.R.R. Tolkien. Seven years later he joined up and served in France and Germany. The bicycle was an appropriate acquisition as his father had a business manufacturing cycle parts and 'trinkets', which covered a host of items such as metal buttons and match holders. (Audrey Trumper)

Is it a fish? Is it a crab? A look of anticipation is on the faces of these young boys in the summer holidays of 1955. I took this photograph on honeymoon – nice to see someone else having a good time too. It was a common sight to see boys fishing with handlines on their annual week at the seaside – which was all most hard-working parents could afford back then. (Albert Couldwell, **Runner Up**)

This is me in my cot when I was about one and a half. My picture is special to me because it shows me as a baby, and when I was born Nelson Mandela was released from prison. (Eleanor Nuttall)

The picture is of interest as it illustrates the changing use of buildings. In 1895, when this picture was taken, the shed in the background was a gymnasium and the open building next to it was the where the boys' lockers were kept. Now it is a modern technology centre. The picture also shows how games have changed. These kind of gymnastic drills are rarely seen today. There are cricket stumps chalked on the wall. Cricket is still played regularly by pupils at the school. (Sophie A. Ibbotson, Ackworth School, **Secondary School Winner**)

'Flower Power.' We were happy, we were young, carefree and twenty. Old chums on holiday for the summer. It was hot and sunny. We swam naked in the sea, a group of about six of us. Oh, happy youth. (Jackie Webb)

'A moment in time'. Sunday 30 May 1999 was the last day of BBC Music Live in Glasgow, and in the city centre at every corner there were bands playing and a wonderful carnival atmosphere. These unknown children were playing with street snakes. To me, although this photograph was taken recently it has a look of early in the century, when the children might have been running with hoops and wearing boots. (Joyce Henry)

My father and me holding a big conger eel, 1994. The picture was taken by my mother in our back garden. This was an important start to my life because my father has taught me how to fish and has given me a gift that I won't forget. Every year I'm progressing towards more advanced fishing. Now in the year 2000 we have entered competitions and have won lots of medals. I love my father and I will follow in his footsteps. I hope our seas will be full of fish in the future. (Martin Christopher, St Osmund's Middle School)

This is a picture of my daughter, Rosie. It was taken at one of our favourite places to walk, the local Dock Museum. I like the photo because Rosie is almost sixteen and soon will be making her own way in life. But as a parent you worry and hope that everything goes well for her. I just want her to know she will always be special to me and my wife Paula. We love you. (Steven Hillman)

A young boy proud with his cycle and in his Sunday best for a photograph – my dad's fashionable dress of the day. (Dorothy Jackson)

Childhood ambition – engine driver. I was about fifteen and a half when this photograph was taken during the first few weeks of my promotion to fireman, getting to grips with my first big locomotive. It was on the 1650 hrs Worcester (stopping all stations) to Gloucester service. Ambition achieved! I became a driver in 1977, but unfortunately retired in December 1999 through ill health. (Howard Griffiths)

My first day at school. A new start in life, a new beginning. The first day of opening the door to a superb education. The first day I walked into the classroom slowly, not knowing what was going to happen. There was my teacher, Mrs Winn, sitting down with a few other of my soon to be classmates and friends. Since then I have enjoyed being at Birkenhead Preparatory School. At the end of my first day I was keener and I enjoyed it instead of being nervous, and I couldn't wait to go back the next day. (Andrew McGibbon, Birkenhead Preparatory School)

My mum when she was one year old. She was sitting in my nan's front garden. This picture is very special because it's of my Mummy and it shows me what she looked like when she was very small. It is important because you can compare the picture to pictures of me and my brother to see who we looked more like. (Conor Brooks, Avonmouth Primary School)

These children are growing up in rural poverty, c. 1900. My great-grandfather worked on a farm near Chipping Norton, Oxfordshire, and at least one of these children is my first cousin once removed (i.e. the grandchild of my great-grandfather). The children are dressed in an assortment of ill-fitting and grubby clothes, bare-footed and bare-legged, with no apparent playthings. The eldest is looking after the younger children and the facial expressions reflect the bleakness of their lives. The agricultural depression (due to poor harvests and cheap imports of wheat and meat) is here given a human face. (Jean Alen)

Boys and girls at Ackworth School in 1902 were taught in separate buildings, the boys on one side of the Green and the girls on the other. The only place they could meet was on the centre path on the Green, and even then they could only meet if they were related. So some people faked family relations with the opposite sex. Today boys and girls are taught together in many schools. (Alex Parker, Ackworth School, **Secondary School Winner**)

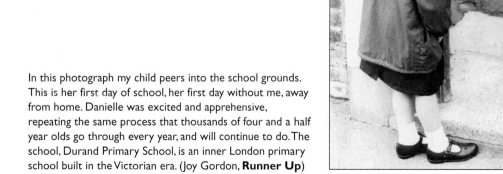

In this photograph my child peers into the school grounds. This is her first day of school, her first day without me, away from home. Danielle was excited and apprehensive, repeating the same process that thousands of four and a half year olds go through every year, and will continue to do. The school, Durand Primary School, is an inner London primary school built in the Victorian era. (Joy Gordon, **Runner Up**)

Birthdays in the 1940s were celebrated with games in the garden and party hats. Just after the war life was returning to normal and rationing was coming to an end. Birthday parties were a big treat and a change to enjoy jelly, blancmange and ice cream. You used to take a basin to the corner shop to collect some ice cream for tea. It's very different to today's birthday parties at McDonald's followed by sleepovers. (Kenneth Reynolds)

This photo was originally sent to my paternal grandmother by a friend, showing her grandson dancing round the maypole. It came to me on the death of my aunt and is one of a large collection of photos taken mainly between about 1910 and 1930. I was fortunate to get them, as my mother rescued them from being destroyed on a bonfire. It will show future generations how children amused themselves at that time, and how they dressed. Dancing round the maypole on 1 May was a long-standing custom in the early twentieth century. (Muriel Tansley)

This picture, taken just before the Second World War, shows my husband David and his best friend Tommy Stockman with their pride and joy: a genuine go-kart made in the approved fashion from orange boxes and old pram wheels. They and the other children played happily and safely all day in the road, because of the total lack of traffic. This photo is also one of the last taken showing the iron railings and gates fronting the houses in the street before they were taken away to help the war effort, sadly never to be replaced. (Gillian May, **Winner**)

My grandma and her brother in Rotherham, South Yorkshire. She told me that one day a man came to the door and asked her mother if her children would like to have their photograph taken sitting in a car (for a charge of one penny!) Gran said it was so exciting because having your photograph taken was very unusual and cars were almost unheard of in her area at this time. When they dashed out, after having been 'got ready', they were very disappointed to see the car was only a cardboard cut-out. Gran was very embarrassed by the whole situation as lots of kids from nearby houses turned out to stand behind the photographer and pull faces at her! (Trevor Haddrell)

When you think of childhood you think of school, but this photo of my aunt and her classmates shows how classrooms have changed. The windows are high so pupils weren't distracted. The walls are tiled and there is no sign of any posters or children's work on display. The pupils are sitting up straight with their hands out of sight behind their backs. The double desks have inkwells. The children don't look very happy, perhaps because any misbehaviour meant a rap across the knuckles with a ruler. (Kenneth Reynolds)

This winter scene of Boxmoor, Hertfordshire, is special to me because it brings back fond memories of my boyhood days when my father made a sledge and pulled me and my sister along this avenue. Whenever I leave my home I see this view, but the snow is left in my childhood, when winters were much colder than now. But to a young boy they were magical times. (Ian Rance)

A photograph probably taken by my mother in 1953, of me and 'The Gang'. The house we lived in had an entry straight from the road at the front. It was in these small areas that we would play endless games of football and cricket. I am clutching the bat after such a match. In the background can be seen the big sister of one of my mates. When we were a little older our parents allowed us to go to the newly created playing field nearby. (Nigel Gooch)

This photograph is special to me because it was taken when my brother was born in 1993. It was taken in a hospital when my brother was less than an hour old. (Samuel Bignell, Charfield Primary School)

Me and my twin sister Maureen aged two. We had both lived at a Dr Barnardo's home at Kelvedon in Essex since we were a week old. Unfortunately my sister had been a fragile child and died of TB at the age of 2½ in 1953. This photo was used with the 'thank you' boxes that raised money for the homes. I remained in care at Kelvedon until 1954 when I was settled with my future parents. (John Osbourne)

This photograph brings back such happy memories of my childhood back in 1935–46. My sister and I were on holiday in Filey where we went every year with the rest of the family, mother, dad and two brothers. We stayed in a boarding house: the owner, Mrs Taylor, ran it. Mother brought the food every day, Mrs Taylor cooked it for a family of six for a week, and the bill for everything came to £6 12s 10½d. I found the bill when my parents passed away. (Ms Thompson)

My dad with his friend Nick Taylor. The fish is a pike weighing 7½ lb and 28½ in long. He caught it under a railway bridge at Three Arches Pond near Stoney Lane in Christchurch, Dorset. He killed it by hitting it on the head with a lump of coal which had rolled down the railway embankment from a steam train. He took the head to St Peter's School to show his class and shared the rest with his family: they said it was delicious. (Edward Hannifan, Ringwood Comprehensive, **Secondary School Winner**)

This is a picture of my son Joe, aged seven, hugging a tree in Kensington Gardens. He has always enjoyed growing things, especially vegetables. I hope that future generations will not forget the importance of trees and other plants, or miss out on the enjoyment there is in growing them. (Joanna Rice)

This photograph encompasses many significant things for this day and age: in the main, children's enjoyment of the fairground, even an age-old traditional sideshow, in contrast with Andrew wearing the fashion of the age – sportswear. (Julian Berry)

I think that this photograph of our daughter Julie happily making a daisy chain perfectly encapsulates the joy and innocence of childhood, which sadly nowadays has been eroded, and is increasingly under attack by today's materialistic and politically correct society. (Ann O'Neil, **Runner Up**)

I particularly like this photograph. The deep concentration on the children's faces, the imagination going through their minds as they play with their medieval soldiers and the closeness and friendship — so far away from today's children with their computers, TV games and electronic toys. (Paul Langford)

Grandad Alan Hibbert took this snap of his three youngest grandchildren Ruth Lord, Victoria and James Hibbert, during a holiday in Keswick in August 1997. The majestic hills behind, with Catbells in the middle, make an interesting backdrop to this very happy picture. You can almost hear the children's laughter. This photo epitomises leisure in the 1990s and the joys of childhood as the little ones play (suitably supervised). (Alan Hibbert)

This young lady is named Stevie Lee Cooke. She was born on Tyneside in England on 11 July 1998. She was so very ill at birth. It was, for some time, touch and go. But with the dedication of our doctors and nurses she is now lively, intelligent and interested in everything. Now she, with her mum and dad, who live and work in Abu Dhabi, United Arab Emirates, has a bright future to look forward to. (B.A. Cooke, **Runner Up**)

This is something you don't see enough of these days. My wife took this photo at the school where she taught in the 1950s. It is her infants class doing PE lessons, learning exercises and balancing on narrow beams, the girl having just gone through the hoop being held by another. Happy days. (Ronald Pears)

I happened to pass this children's group at play, I had my camera at the ready and took a shot. These are working-class children in a quarrying village (Trefor). Note the old houses and tiny frontages and garden. The background is Yr Eifi, where granite was quarried. (Gwyneth Jones)

I love looking at this photograph of Boy Scouts on a Remembrance Day parade, at Biddulph, Stoke-on-Trent, Remembrance Sunday and the Boy Scout movement have both become part of British history and way of life. The smiles on their faces as they proudly parade their banner is a joy to see, as they show not only their willingness to honour and respect the memory of those who gave their lives for others, but also their dedication to helping less fortunate members of their troop to take part. (Melvyn Hughes)

My two younger sons, Christopher Carl, three and a half years old, and Jan Conrad, aged two, out to enjoy the snow – seldom a feature in East Kent winters any more. Global warming brings us rain and wind now. They are wearing all in one boiler-type suits made by me from cut-down overcoats, bought at the ever useful local jumble sales, which provided an endless supply of clothes, toys and books as they grew up.
(Ruth Nicol)

Roger Andrew was a district officer in what was then Rhodesia. He was on leave with his family, staying in his mother's house in Oxford. They had just bought an electric train which had to be battery operated in order to work in the 'bush', and were trying it out for the first time.
(Roger Minshull)

This is a depiction of all our idyllic dreams of our youth. Children playing happily and innocently on the sea wall: no traffic problems, no crowds, just simplicity and innocence. This is the childhood we all dreamed we had thirty or forty years ago. It is a depiction of a past era, but pictured in recent times. (Anthony Coxall)

Me and my parents on holiday in Blackpool in 1949. My father was a miner and to us 'ordinary folk' it was like a dream come true. We stayed in a caravan and unlike most today had to collect all our water from a tap which can be seen on the wall behind us. Although my parents were only in their thirties the style of dress in those days seems to make them look older. I was four years old and a whole new world was opened to me that year. I still remember the joy I felt. (Marlene Jenkins)

A story from the *Rupert Bear Annual*, being read to my cousin Barry and myself by Uncle Derrick, Christmas 1950. The adventures of Rupert and friends entertained us then and have remained firm favourites with collectors today. Storytelling was a normal activity by the adults of the family. *Listen with Mother* on the radio, clockwork trains and Meccano sets kept us amused. We had no television in the house. Seems strange to recall nowadays at the height of IT. (Nigel Gooch, **Winner**)

I never knew my father, I only know a name. I was lucky as I knew my natural mother and liked her. I was unlucky in that one day I was removed from the mother figure who had cared for me from the point of my illegitimate birth and whom I had grown to love deeply. Here I skip easily between both mothers. Later a tug-of-love ensued which was painful for us all. My experience is common among those tagged 'war baby'. Illegitimacy no longer hides: its stigma is destroyed. I search still for my father. (Jacqueline Bompas)

My first set of wheels! It appears that an uncle of mine (who was a cabinet-maker by trade) made me a horse on wheels. I remember having hours of enjoyment riding and pushing it – a very simple wooden toy must have meant a great deal to me at that age. As far as I can recall, none of my friends had a horse like mine! (Ian Wyn Jones)

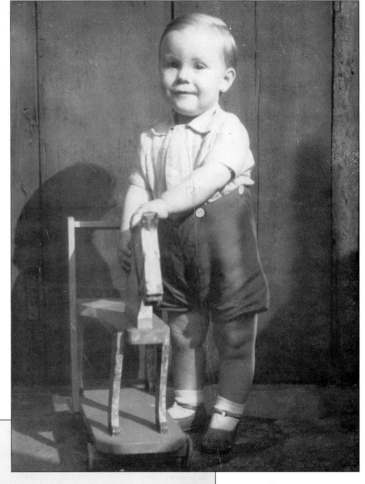

Local boys sitting on two 'gambos', as they were called. The gambos were made from old wheels and a plank of wood. It was great fun racing down the hills of this mining valley. (Glyndwr Hughes, **ntl Entrant**)

The day was the feast of Corpus Christi, celebrated by the Catholic Church since 1264. Processions took place all over the world and every Catholic schoolchild in Cardiff and surrounding areas looked forward to walking through the civic centre to a mass in the castle grounds, followed by a huge picnic with family and friends. Sadly the event was scaled down in about 1977 much to the disappointment of the older Irish/Catholic community. Nothing will ever compare to that early event. Happy days! (Barbara-Ann Jenkins)

This was a photograph that I took in 1982, while I was working on a voluntary basis at the Merseyside Trade Union unemployed resource centre in Liverpool. It is of one of the children in the day nursery at the centre, which was primarily to assist unemployed parents to attend courses at the centre, in order to improve their job prospects. The child was playing at dressing up, and I was struck by her particularly piercing blue eyes. (Alan Reekie)

Watching Punch and Judy shows always held a fascination – perhaps now replaced by computer games and TV – but in the past a good Punch and Judy show always attracted a large audience. (Donald Morris)

Halcyon days of childhood, where playgrounds were part of our heritage. Our children were safe, happy and thoroughly enjoyed the camaraderie and happiness of playing together. The three brothers are being pushed on the roundabout by the little girl cousin. The mother of the little girl happily watches on, while the mother of the three boys is taking the photograph. Oh, such happy days. The playgrounds are gone, but there are always children needing somewhere to play and enjoy the simple pleasures of life as part of growing up. (Pamela Rose Strange)

This is my cousin Stephen Thomas Cox in a wonderful car, c. 1958. It was similar to the cars that were on fairground roundabouts, but at least this one could be driven. It had its own little garage and was a real beauty. The registration number had Stephen's initials and the number of his house. When he moved house the registration number was changed to match his new address. If they had kept the car it would have been worth a lot of money today. (Andy Beech)

This photograph was taken during a street party for the Queen's Coronation in 1953. It has personal value as my father who was eleven and his two brothers are in it, and there are very few photographs of them as children. It has historical value because it shows the different clothing that came just after the war finished. It also shows how close the community was, and shows future generations a way of life and style of housing that have virtually disappeared. No one in that street had a television or a motor car, which is unheard of today in Britain. (Antonia Marsh)

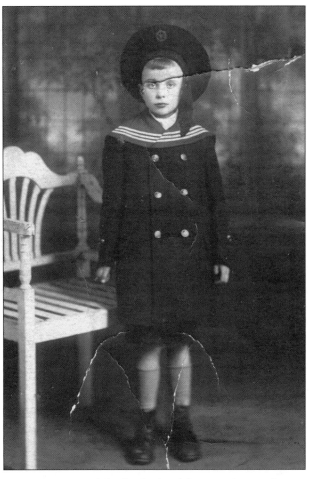

I am the last one left of a family of fourteen. I am eighty-six years old. We were a poor family, but if you had a sailor suit like the one I am wearing you were well off. (Robert Brooke)

Santa's gifts were simple and inexpensive – a nurse's outfit and a rag doll – but joy shines out of my daughter's face. In the innocence of childhood she cuddled her 'Sammy', with no thoughts of the racial prejudice that is now attached to such a toy. (Margaret Wilkinson)

This photograph was taken in July 1914 only weeks before the start of the First World War. It shows a school outing from Govan, Glasgow, to the seaside at Largs. In the photograph are my grandmother, Annie Duncan (wearing a white scarf), and her two youngest daughters, Marie aged five sitting on her left, and Nessie aged two sitting on her lap proudly holding a bucket. Nessie was my mother. This picture illustrates what was probably one of the last such happy occasions for some considerable time, as the war put an end to outings like this. (Celia Voller)

Four lads from Liverpool changed the musical world. Here is a picture of my brother Philip aged four years and eight months in August 1964 – the height of Beatlemania. The Beatles were bigger than God, according to John Lennon anyway. They were one of this country's biggest exports and something which I think English people should be proud of. Nowadays people from all over the world visit Liverpool to see Penny Lane and Strawberry Fields. They certainly had a massive impact on this four-year-old standing in his very own Penny Lane with his new Beatles haircut. (Beverley Smith)

Somewhere in my photo collection I have a snap like this of me as a child walking down an English lane with my mother, and another of my daughter at the same age walking down a road with me. Looking at this snap of my son's wife Tracy and their daughter Ellen I realise that, although our family history is inevitably changing because they have gone to start a new life in Australia, the photo might be in another country but it's still another mother and daughter of our family walking down a road together. (Millie Richardson)

'Open wide, this won't hurt': a class of boys at Pocklington County School, Yorkshire, in 1920, in a performance of a play involving dentists. Wilfred Newsome, my father, was the 'patient' in the third chair from the right. (David Newsome)

The photograph was taken in the summer of 1999 at St Joseph's School, Blaydon, Tyne & Wear. It is the school's annual sports day and includes my son David aged six, and his classmates ready to start the race. I think this photo sums up the carefree fun of a British summer's day. (Gillian Lauder)

The original of this, my mother's copy, was lost years ago. I last saw it in 1969 or 1970. When she left home in 1973 all trace of her was removed from the house by my dad. Last year, while using a friend's bathroom, I saw it reproduced as a poster on the back of his door. I recognised it immediately and he gave it to me on the spot. My aunt without prompting picked out both of her sisters in an instant. (Kevin Wilton, **Runner Up**)

We were trying to earn a living as craft workers, and were very hard up. The cottages emptied for redevelopment were rented as short life studios by artists and the like, who would then live in them. We weren't supposed to but it was very cheap, 50p a week! A happy, creative time. Outside, the cold wind continued. Always ratcheting up a notch and never slackening off. I worried that Ian would not reach maturity because of it. He did – he is now a biologist and research scientist and still loved above everything else by his parents. (Andrew McLeod, **Runner Up**)

This photograph was taken in August 1971 of my niece Laura at the 'Auld Lammas Fair', Ballycastle, Co. Antrim. The fair dates back to 1606 and was principally agricultural. Today it hosts stalls from potatoes to brass candlesticks. People come from as far as Scotland to buy and sell their wares. As children we always looked forward to this annual event. My niece was three years old then and was rather taken aback when a local street photographer thrust a small capuchin monkey into her arms. Her expression is more bemused than amused. (Lynn Kilpatrick)

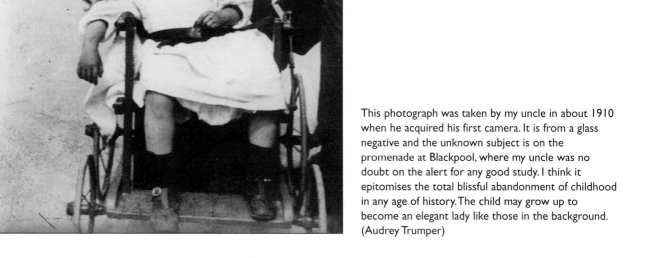

This photograph was taken by my uncle in about 1910 when he acquired his first camera. It is from a glass negative and the unknown subject is on the promenade at Blackpool, where my uncle was no doubt on the alert for any good study. I think it epitomises the total blissful abandonment of childhood in any age of history. The child may grow up to become an elegant lady like those in the background. (Audrey Trumper)

My tenth birthday party in the garden of my parents' then home at Wigginton, near York. It features four friends – Andrew Knight, Andrew Appleton, Richard Baker and Paul Knight – my brother Simon, sister Anna, and me. One of the most striking things about the picture is the different expressions and poses adopted by my friends, brother, sister and me. A further detail is that it shows the sorts of clothes children aged seven, eight, ten and eleven wore in 1977. In particular, how many children would wear a tie to a party today? (Paul Jobson)

This is me in 1950 with my doll's pram. Like many of my toys it was home made. My parents renovated an ancient pram body with paint and American cloth. New wheels were bought by post. My mother made bedding and a neighbour knitted an outfit for the baby doll, who wet her nappy when fed! I still have these, also my doll's cot, doll's house, and other toys made lovingly when I was in bed. I probably appreciated my toys more than today's children who demand – and often get – the latest fashionable toy and then tire of it quickly. (Dorothy Rand)

The cottage in Fordham, Cambridgeshire, (later condemned) which the family rented (2s 6d per week) and was evacuated to. There were seven sisters and seven brothers in the family. The men went to war and the women lived in the two-bedroom cottage. The photo was taken by Marty Fresco (later MBE), renowned Fleet Street photographer at the age of twenty-one. The family kept the cottage on after the war until 1956. During the war it housed fifteen children aged under one to twelve and five or six women. The toilet was a hole in the ground and water was collected from a pump. (Michael Fresco)

The west end of Newcastle was, and is, 'deprived'. Note the cotton dresses. Yet childhood always provided fun and laughter. (Bernard Kat, **Runner Up**)

In the photo it is my third birthday. I have two cousins on my left and two of my friends on my right. This photo is special to me because it shows me having a great time with my friends and family. It was taken in 1993. (Leanne Bleaken, Charfield Primary School)

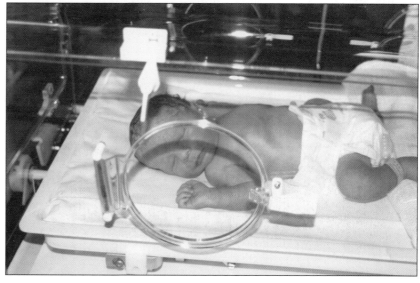

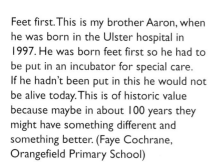

Feet first. This is my brother Aaron, when he was born in the Ulster hospital in 1997. He was born feet first so he had to be put in an incubator for special care. If he hadn't been put in this he would not be alive today. This is of historic value because maybe in about 100 years they might have something different and something better. (Faye Cochrane, Orangefield Primary School)

A group of children, including my late mother, in the playground of Tooting Graveney School, south London, c. 1924. They were involved with May Day celebrations, dancing around the maypole – a pagan festival that marked the beginning of summer and continued into the early 1950s. As far as I am aware, it is no longer practised in schools today. (Trevor Smithers)

I chose this photo because it reminds me of my grandad (the one without the hat) and reminds me of my own childhood Scout camps, which were great fun though normally wet! Fortunately we didn't wear shorts and big hats! This photo was taken in the early 1930s and my grandad was Scout leader. He was in Scouting all of his life and was awarded one of the highest honours in Scouting, the silver acorn. It is nice to think that nearly seventy years later, in the new millennium, Scouting is still enjoyed by many throughout the world; all that has changed is the uniform. (Sam Clarke, Coopers Company & Coborn School)

Four people standing in a garden in their respective Scout/Guide uniforms. From left to right they are my grandad, Brian Rankin, my great-aunt Eveleen and my two great-uncles, Neal and Dennis. My grandad has died, Eveleen is still alive and my great-uncles both died in the Second World War. The men were members of the 78th Scout group. The photograph was taken around 1931–2 in the garden of 11 Hopefield Avenue in North Belfast. The house is still there. (Timothy Rankin, Royal Belfast Academic Institution, **Secondary School Winner**)

My father, Brian Watson, was born in 1947. His parents met at the end of the war and were married in 1946. Many men who had been in the forces during the war settled down and started families when the war was over. This meant there was a huge baby-boom. The children here are all baby-boomers; because so many children were born after the war they had to put up with several disadvantages. Classes at school were big and it was harder to pass exams like the eleven-plus and to get into university. Later there was increased pressure on housing and jobs. The baby-boomers were the young people who lived through the 'Swinging Sixties'. (Alex Watson, Danes Hill School, **Primary School Winner**)

Sand is great for playing in! A young boy of nursery age plays in the sand with toy cars and plastic buckets and spades. In the background are pictures of the seaside to widen the child's experience or remind him of what he already knows. The photograph was taken by a Y6 pupil, and is one of a collection of photographs made for a head teacher who was to retire. We have been using a photograph of a Victorian schoolroom to learn about education in the nineteenth century. Perhaps someone will learn about nursery education in the year 2000 when they see this one! (St Dominic's Catholic Primary School)

This is my dad at his school, Lightcliff Primary, in Yorkshire. He is on the bottom row, right hand corner. All the boys wore ties, except for one. Nearly all the girls have pinafores with cardigans. My dad said there were no school uniforms, they just wore what was put out for them. Nowadays, we get told off if we don't wear the school dress code. My dad got hit once on the hand in primary school. We don't get hit at all – it's against the law. (Kristine Catherine Jones, West Calder High School)

This is a picture of my mum, grandad, Auntie Margaret, and their teddy bears. Mum is on the left. This year Mum was forty-six and Grandad was seventy. I don't know how old Margaret is. It is a happy family photo showing how close and loving parents and children can be. (Sam Brushett, Edgworth Primary School)

My grandfather, Cyril Davies, is sitting in the front row, far left. He is with the other members of his Bagilt School football team, which in 1930 had won a competition against other school teams. They had won a large shield and a small medal, which each boy is wearing. This is an important historical photo because it shows that schoolboys enjoyed football, and that matches were organised for them. It also shows us how the players dressed for the game, and how teachers dressed, and that hairstyles were neat. (Stuart Davies, Flint High School, **Secondary School Winner**)

To begin the school's centenary celebrations we invited Miss Dorothy Lewis to school. She taught at the school from 1945 to 1960 and was 100 years of age. She is pictured here with the youngest child in the school. Unfortunately Miss Lewis died in June 2000, but when she visited she was an inspiration to pupils and staff alike. (Reception Class, Gnoll Primary School)

This photo was taken on our first proper family holiday. We were very excited because it was the day of the eclipse, and we were waiting for the sky to go black as we were staying in Devon. We bought the gold pompons from Morris Minor's kids' club and thought they looked great as shiny scarecrow hair. There are palm trees in the picture as it is quite warm, and they can grow in Devon valleys. (Richard Oliver Caddocks, Gorse Covert Primary School)

This photo was taken in Yarmouth in 1966. It shows my mum and her older brother. My mum is wearing a dress her mum knitted for her. People did a lot more knitting in those days. You are no longer allowed to take photos with animals wearing clothes. (Sophie Tristham, Gayton Junior School)

This photograph is of personal value to me because it shows my mum and uncle when they were small. They were playing with the water. This is special because it shows my family history and my grandchildren will be able to see what their great-grandmother looked like when she was little. (Katie Ryan, Hagbourn CE Primary School)

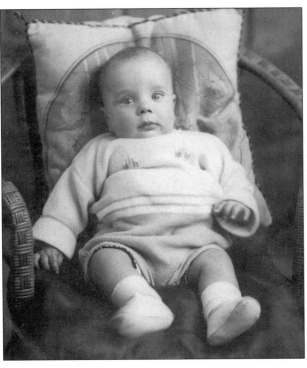

This is a picture of my grandad who was brought up in the East End of London. He was five months old when the photo was taken. I think people in the future would like to see what clothes babies wore in 1933. (Gina Baldwin, Edward Francis Junior School)

This photograph was taken in 1959 by a street photographer. It shows my father, Paul Lewis (aged five), hand in hand with my great-grandfather, Robert Noble (fifty), strolling along Royal Avenue, Belfast. My grandfather worked as a fitter in Harland & Wolff shipyard all his life. They got on very well together and often went into town on Saturdays. A scribble on the back of the picture by my great-grandfather reads, 'note Paul's wristlet watch (toy)', which he had bought for him earlier that afternoon. Notice the buildings behind them, which were replaced by today's Castle Court Shopping Centre. (Adam Lewis, Royal Belfast Academic Institution, **Secondary School Winner**)

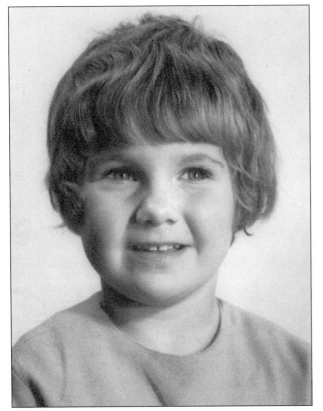

This picture of my mum was taken in 1967 when she was four years old. It reflects my family history because a lot of people say that my mum and I look alike although I don't think we do, because when my mum was this age she looked a lot like my sister did when she was that age. This black and white photo was taken by a professional photographer. I think it cost quite a lot of money. I think the '60s would have been a good era to live in because it was fun. (Kay Jordan, Priory High School)

This picture is of my mum's family on Whit Sunday in 1963. All the family are in their best clothes, as was traditional on Whit Sunday, which is a festival on the seventh Sunday (fiftieth day) after Easter, commemorating the descent of the Holy Spirit on the apostles as they celebrated the ancient Jewish feast of Shabuoth. Whit Sunday isn't celebrated any more by most people. It was an important day where children got new clothes or wore their best. Children looked forward to Whit Sunday. This shows how times change. (Fay Grace George, Intake High School)

This image was taken around 1923 in the playground of Tooting Graveney School, south London, and shows a group of children, including my late mother. They were involved with May Day celebrations (dancing around the maypole), a Celtic festival that marked the beginning of summer, and continued into the early 1950s. As far as I am aware, it is no longer practised in schools today. (Trevor Smithers)

Ballyholey was a rural school and the playground was made of stones, gravel and clay packed together. Note the wellington boots and dirty shoes. The building in the background was the boys' dry toilet. This photograph will be of interest to future generations because it shows the style of clothes worn by rural children in the late 1950s. There are more children in my Primary 7 class today than there were in this whole school. My mum and aunt are both in this photo. (Adam Caldwell, New Buildings Primary School)

The photo is of my football team. This was the last photo with my friends and the last photo of my football team because it was our last match. I think people might be interested in it because it shows us that we should work as a team. I might never see my friends again because they might move away. When I get older I can see what I looked like, and what my friends looked like. It will act as a memory. (Juneid Patel, Sharples School)

The picture was taken in January 1971 in London at Trafalgar Square. In the picture is my mum when she was eight, the same age I am now, and also my grandad who died before I was born. My mum and her sister had the day off school to go to London. They went by train and it was the first time she had gone on a train. I chose this photograph because it will be nice to show my children one day. It is also funny to see my mum with a pigeon on her head. (Kate Wyness, Somerset Bridge School)

A group of Loughborough PE students during Rag Week, 1968. They chose to have a game of five-a-side football with a giant ball. They raised a large sum of money and gave it to local hospitals. Rag Week is a college tradition where large groups of students come together and raise money for their local community. It makes students aware of the needs of the local community, and introduces the idea that raising money can be fun. (Daisy Fisher, St Paul's Catholic College, **Secondary School Winner**)

fashion

Me and my mother, who wore her hair in this style for over thirty years. I couldn't understand how her hair grew upwards unlike mine. If I ever lost her I looked up for the giant candyfloss of hair and I always found her. It wasn't until I was nineteen that I saw her with it down at the local hairdresser, before it was piled up and lacquered. This lasted a week. It was so hard it never moved. When down, it touched her bum. (W. Johnstone, **Runner Up**)

My mum and dad roughly nine months after they met. Just by looking at the photo, you can see that it was taken in the '70s. I know this because of the type of clothing they are wearing. My dad has a typical man's shirt on. It's reasonably tight, with a retro type of pattern. My mum, on the other hand, is wearing a purple dress and a lilac and white shirt, both made by her older sister, Anne. The hairstyles are also another give-away – my dad's especially, with his sideburns. Altogether a truly wonderful photo, which tells so much, it's a great picture to keep! (Kim Stephen, Bridge of Don Academy, **Secondary School Winner**)

This is a photograph of me in the summer of 1999. I went to a fancy dress party as Baby Spice. The Spice Girls were brilliant and made some great records, which sometimes got to number one in the charts. They also had a big influence on fashion because lots of people wanted to dress just like them. (Sarah Ketteringham, Ashville College)

Female staff at my school in the nineteenth century. They all look really miserable, but it isn't just because they are at school. They had to hold their pose for a long time while the image was taken. You can tell this because a breeze has disturbed a bush in the background. Future generations might be interested to see how such an image was taken with such a slow shutter speed. Their clothes are quite different from today's styles. They are wearing crinolines to make their skirts look full and all their clothes are made of heavy material. All of their bodies are completely covered, except for hands and heads. The flourishing leaves behind them show that it was probably quite warm. It must have been very uncomfortable to wear such clothes in the summer – and this was a time before deodorants! (Keeley Fawcett, Ackworth School, **Secondary School Winner**)

My mother and her sister (wearing typical 1960s clothes!) at Butlin's in Barry in 1968. At this time Butlin's was extremely popular as it had not been open long. It was the place to go! In those days Butlin's was seen as a holiday. Now it's a place to go when the weather's nice. (Jessica Delahaye, Aberdare Girls' School, **Secondary School Winner**)

At this time cricket was a big sport. The picture shows the team wearing waistcoats and ties as though they play cricket in them. Cricket was first introduced at Ackworth in the 1840s; by the 1870s it was an established sport. Some masters at the school were concerned about its influence upon the boys. One said: 'excellent a game as cricket is, it has its dangers. . . . Let the strictest impartiality mark either side, let victory be proclamed without unkind exaltation: let defeat be borne with good tempered cheerfulness.' It is interesting to read these concerns at a time when match-fixing dominates the game. Although cricket was very popular at this time, it is less popular in schools today. (Stephen Spurr & James Birdsall, Ackworth School, **Secondary School Winner**)

This photograph was taken in 1939 and shows a pupil sitting outside wearing roller skates. Historically it is interesting to note that roller-skating was a hobby in the 1930s. Today some pupils carry on the tradition by riding skateboards in the same area. The graffiti on the gatepost can still be seen today, but some more might have been added since the picture was taken. (Jack Sheard, Ackworth School, **Secondary School Winner**)

This photograph is personal as well as historic. All these people are now in their mid-fifties, and the lady at the back gives some idea of the fashions at the time. My sister is also in the picture, second from the left.
(Eric Forshaw)

These take me back to my teens and the '70s era of glitter pop and rock. I remember the mini skirts, hot pants, afro hair, hippies, round collared shirts and kipper ties. But mostly I remember the good times and the music. In the year 2000 there are '70s musicals and revivals everywhere. The younger generation now enjoy the rhythm and excitement of the music, which is so upbeat and memorable: it leaves you with a 'feel good' feeling – definitely a part of fashion history. (Lynne Torson)

My mother posing in a park flower garden. It shows the fashions of the 1920s, with the large hat and feather. (Ronald Pears)

At first glance you might think this is a middle-aged lady. She is in fact a relative of mine, Ellen Reed, and she was in her early twenties. The photograph was taken sometime during the First World War. It is the fashion which makes her look older. Her long coat and skirt and the high-necked fancy blouse cover most of the body. The fur stole and the hat seem old fashioned too, yet it was the height of fashion and these would have been her best clothes. (Kaye Cameron, Duncanrig Secondary School, **Secondary School Winner**)

My mum and Maggie standing in a hotel foyer in Manchester. This photo is interesting to us mainly because of the hairstyles. My mum is now a brunette. What also amused us were the stripy curtains; how times have changed. This will be of interest to future generations because it shows how fashions have changed and maybe even returned. (Alice Winter, Clifton High School)

This photograph has caused some amusement in my family. It is a picture of a ladies' picnic in a charabanc. The ladies were customers of the Blacksmiths Arms, Helsby Street, Ardwick, Manchester. The area was cleared in the 1960s. You have a photograph here of working-class women presumably in their Sunday best. Apparently the hats at least are fashionable for the period. I cannot remember my mother mentioning whether the photo was taken pre- or post-liquid refreshment. Some of the ladies appear rather stiff, hard, no-nonsense characters, with hearts of gold no doubt! (John Brian Speet)

My great-great-grandfather and grandmother (Talbot), and great-grandfather (little boy with hat on) with his older brother. This family photograph printed on glass is probably one of the very earliest of its type and may have been taken by Fox Talbot, who was a distant relative. I think the child's trolley and the clothes they are wearing are of particular interest. Considering the negative is 150 years old, it shows the quality of photography at that time. (Roger Aspray, **Winner**)

Looking at this photograph of my grandmother, Norah Crosby (right) and her cousin Nora Hanson (aged two) in 1906, makes me glad that I live in the twenty-first century, when we enjoy so much more freedom in the clothes we wear. The outfits that the girls are wearing were handmade by members of the family, which was the norm. They are rather formal, highly decorative and the height of fashion, though my grandmother looks less than convinced! One has only to consider the present-day variety of materials, fastenings and styles to understand why I would not wish to change places. (Kate Hopper, **Runner Up**)

This is a picture of my ancestors, 1910. My mother is the baby on the extreme right sitting on my grandmother's knee. My grandmother was widowed a couple of months before this photograph hence the black outfit and the solemn expression. Her sister is at the other end of the row with the very young baby on her knee. Her husband is behind her: he is Tom Clough who was a legendary Northumbrian piper. He made pipes and played them and also played the fiddle and wrote music – in spite of being completely deaf as a result of his work as a shotfirer in the coal mines. His name is still held in high esteem by pipers today. He and his wife, Nancy, supported my mother and grandmother as there were no state benefits then. (Kenneth Morton)

This photo was taken on 11 September 1971 at Merthyr Tydfil Register Office. My auntie is the one getting married, with her sister standing next to her, and my mother is the one on the far right. I think future generations will be interested in this because they can see what wedding dresses and fashions were like in the 1970s. (Rebecca Forrester, St John Baptist High School)

This photograph shows the style, fashions and attitude of the 1960s era. Recreated under studio conditions and developed in black and white, it captures something of the period. (Jane Robertshaw)

A new print technology pioneered by GPL printers of Edenbridge, Kent, was used on exciting fabrics and designs produced by London College of Fashion students, to create a photofabric garment of distinction. (Peter Watson)

My mother, Mrs Gladys Valley (née Whitely), in 1947 at the Scarborough Butlin's holiday camp, which has recently closed. My mother was a waitress there and this photo was taken when she was off duty. Notice the clothes and style of her hair, which were typical of those years. (Rosetta Martigan)

The group are taking part in Belper Carnival, Derbyshire, representing Christchurch. My husband's Aunty Winnie is in the foreground, holding a cup and saucer. She is twenty-two years old, the year 1936. 'Please help the hospitals' is as appropriate today as it was then. Perhaps it should have read 'please help our mill', as Jebediah Strutt's Mill, built in the industrial revolution and Belper's heart (eventually the English Sewing Cotton Company), closed ten years ago. Winnie worked there until she retired at sixty. She is now eighty-six years old and still regularly attends Christchurch. (Hazel White)

A wedding photograph of my grandmother and grandfather in 1904. I had never seen this picture before, until my mother recently moved from her home and I discovered this and another at the bottom of a drawer while sorting through her belongings. It is obvious from their condition that they had never been hung. I love the lace dresses and fresh rose bouquets. It is interesting that in an age of social decorum and correctness none of the wedding photographs which I have seen include the parents of the bride and groom. (Caroline Bagias)

My daughter and I were visiting Edinburgh Festival on 24 August 1998. It was my birthday. As we turned a street corner we met this young traveller and his dog. The 'photo shoot' cost me £1 and a cigarette! We were both in stitches over the whole incident: a birthday I will always remember. I have seen many a mohican haircut in the past – but a punk dog: a useful reference for both past and future fashion study, perhaps. (Nicole Godden)

Two girls from Manchester posing on my BSA 250 motorcycle. They were staying at the same boarding house in the summer of 1956 in Douglas, Isle of Man. It shows the hairstyles and dress fashions of the '50s. (Ronald Pears)

This photograph speaks for itself. Taken only three years ago, it illustrates the type of clothes worn by the modern generation. Probably in ten to fifteen years' time these young girls will look back at this photograph and say, 'Did I wear that then?' On the day this photograph was taken it was typical carnival weather – heavy clouds, strong wind and depressing rain. However, it didn't damp the spirits of these youngsters. (Derek Harding)

These two punks were spotted in London, February 1980. Teen rebellion against the fashion and music of the day prompted punk which became popular in the late '70s and early '80s. Punk fashion attracted attention and it shocked people – they hated it. For this reason it became cool and it gave the youths a whole new world and political philosophy along with a classless society. (Andrew Halling, **Sky Digital Winner**)

Future shock one – twenty-first century girls. I took this yesterday, but it already looks dated. This summer's look has a shelf life of about five minutes. It's already impossible to believe that anybody actually wore that rucksack and redundant scarf, or rode the ridiculous beribboned scooter. A brilliant conception from the marketing boys: 'Let's sell them a totally useless way of getting around – something like the Sinclair C5, but slower and less glamorous; and let's call it "Turbo", because it's very nearly as fast as walking.' The only timeless aspect is the animation and poise of the subjects. (John Carroll, **Runner Up**)

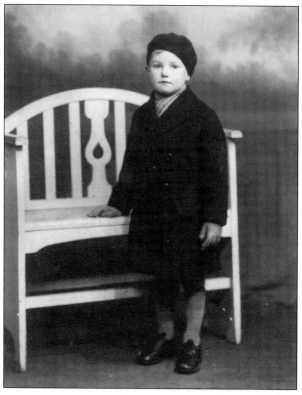

A special photograph of my grandmother Faith and her younger brother Cyril. It is a very important photograph to me because it is one of the few pictures I have of my grandmother, who I never had the chance to meet. My relatives are dressed in a formal fashion, as was expected of children in that time. Children were also supposed to remain clean, tidy and well behaved. Young boys wore girls'-style clothing and golden curls were highly desirable! (Chloe Seddon)

A typical studio photo of the 1930s. It shows me as a four-year-old dressed for colder weather, with overcoat, scarf, beret and gloves. The gloves were small kidskin gloves which my father bought from a company traveller (reps they call them now), and are miniature men's gloves used to show buyers the quality and workmanship of their goods. (Ronald Pears)

An annual outing to Southend, Essex, of workers in a cigarette factory called Miranda's Dreams in London. This will be of interest to future generations as it shows a method of transport in 1920 and the fashions of the time for both sexes for a range of age groups. The dress code of that era for a day at the seaside is very different to today; even the younger members of the group wore formal dress. This is of personal interest to me as the factory was owned by my uncle, who is standing centre in front of the coach and my parents Ben and Jane Levy, left back, who worked there before their marriage in 1925. The lady centre back is my grandmother, who at the date of the photo would have been in her sixties. (Cyril Levy, **Winner**)

A friend of mine, Joy, when she was eighteen, dressed to go to a formal dinner dance, in 1951. Disco styles and the dances were quieter then than they are today. (Elizabeth Pears)

This photograph of me was taken in 1954, four years old, shopping with my mother and father. It portrays the fashion of the day, long double- or single-breasted wool coats with large lapels and brogue shoes. It would not be out of place now: what goes around comes around as they say. (Keith Harris)

In the 1940s to 1950s nylon stockings were scarce and expensive, so small workshops were set up to invisibly mend stockings. The girls in the photo worked in one of these workshops in Carlisle. The sign to the top right of the door showing a dog leaping up and laddering a lady's stockings says Hosiery Repairs. (Ronald Pears)

Found among the family negative collection, stuffed in a box, this photograph, possibly shot by my dad Frank Warren, shows the style of the era. Attitude, dress, even hairstyles, reflect an age still in living memory but long gone in reality. Not knowing who is in it or where it was taken leaves the imagination to fill in the blanks of the brief moment in time. (Graham M. Warren)

This is a photograph of me in 1985 outside my favourite pub, the Sound and Vision in London's Dean Street, which I had been frequenting with my friends for years. It was full of punky, gothy, skinhead people who liked to watch the video jukebox. A change of ownership resulted in an attempt to smarten up the place, with leaflets announcing an imminent name change to the Bath House and new bright decor. Despite being a well-behaved regular I was still banned for my appearance. (Gary Simmons)

Holiday attire in the '30s! My brother Ron, on the right, aged nearly seven, and me on the left, aged eight. We were spending a fortnight's holiday with our parents. This photograph should be of considerable interest to present and future generations as it shows the formal manner in which small schoolboys were expected to dress while on their summer holidays, including of course the regulation school cap. (Cyril Kellman, **Runner Up**)

My wife and me before we went out to a dinner dance on Boxing Day evening, 1958. We were just courting then and this was our first big night out, all formal dress. We celebrated our ruby wedding just before the end of the century. (Ronald Pears)

These two ladies are dressed to impress! I photographed them as they left their coach. I like this picture a lot because they look so relaxed, drinking wine and looking forward to an enjoyable day in the sunshine. (Michael Nulty)

One of the last pictures taken of Miss Alice James at Ty-Trist Colliery, Tredegar. Miss James was employed as a cleaner at the colliery, but she had spent most of her working life in the South Wales coalfield. She was awarded the British Empire Medal in 1948 for a lifetime of faithful service in the coal industry. Incidentally, she did not dress up for this occasion. The feathered hat, shawl and black dress were part of her everyday working gear. (Derek Harding)

My mother made me a new dress every year for the Sunday school anniversary – this was the 1955 model. My dresses were always extremely pretty, in pink, blue, turquoise or mauve satin or taffeta, with matching hair ribbons. This dress had frills and rosebud trimming. My ringlets were produced by rags being wound in overnight – torture to lie on – and the wave on my brow by curling tongs heated in the coal fire. Children have more carefree clothes and hairstyles nowadays. (Dorothy Rand)

My ex-girlfriend Deb getting ready for a night out, 1984. Her style is probably best described as gothic punk inspired by the '70s punk group Siouxsie and the Banshees. Some of the bands we saw in that year were Test Department, Gary Glitter, Status Quo, Manowar, Wasp, Thor and Saxon. They were hardly goth/punk bands, but we crossed over before the term became accepted to describe the then imminent punk/metal crossover that produced such bands as Metallica. (Gary Simmons)

Young Maureen couldn't resist joining her grandma for a holiday photo. This shows the typical older woman's reluctance to wear anything other than her usual clothes at the seaside, the only concession being white canvas plimsolls. Maureen is wearing rubber paddling shoes, standard children's seaside protection in the 1930s and not very comfortable. Now seventy-four herself, she is much less inhibited in her dress and younger in outlook. (Maureen Whitby)

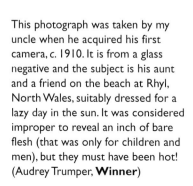

This photograph was taken by my uncle when he acquired his first camera, c. 1910. It is from a glass negative and the subject is his aunt and a friend on the beach at Rhyl, North Wales, suitably dressed for a lazy day in the sun. It was considered improper to reveal an inch of bare flesh (that was only for children and men), but they must have been hot! (Audrey Trumper, **Winner**)

My parents on their wedding day. They were married in Carlisle in 1964 and their clothes are a good example of the fashion trends of that era. As you can see by the haircut my father was a bit of a teddy boy! They lived in Carlisle for all of their married life until my mother died in 1998. My father still lives there in the same house today. (Nigel Boyd)

My grandparents' wedding at the turn of the century. They didn't have very much money and were working class. I don't know how much the hat would have cost then but it would cost a fortune to buy now. My grandmother was only twenty-one years of age and yet the dress was so formal and restricting. She was as slim as modern fashion models. (Margaret Wilkinson)

The occasion of the wedding of Evelyn Webster, sister of the then owner of Battle Abbey, Lucy Webster, to Charles Harbord. Lucy is on the left. At this time the abbey, in Sussex, was a school and the headmistress (Mrs Jacobi) and the governors kindly allowed the reception to be held there. I am the smallest train-bearer on the extreme right. This photograph was taken by Graphic Photo Union of 200 Grays Inn Road, London, WC1. (Tacina Rae-Smith, **Runner Up**)

My cousin Jean was trying to remove a family photo from a frame when she found this being used as backing. The chap on the right is my great-grandfather, John Beech, working at a brickmaker's in Ruabon, Wales. At Ruabon Library a booklet on local brickmakers shows a photo taken in 1902 with men in similar outfits. After being hidden for fifty years, the photograph is fortunately in good condition. Despite working with clay, the employees had to dress respectably. John later became a police constable with Flintshire police force. (Andy Beech, **ntl Entrant**)

Three generations of one family. Great-grandma was very imposing (born in the mid-nineteenth century), grandma (born 1876) and mother (born 1912). This shows women's fashions of the time, how children were dressed and also the family's poor background. My mother recently passed away aged eighty-seven (in December 1999) but told me stories of her mother's life (she died in 1963). They were stoical and hardworking, but always cheerful. They were a product of their times but enjoyed the twentieth century also. They were all true Britons. (Jean Moore)

The photo shows my mother, extreme right, back row, who was not happy with heights but did her bit towards the war effort driving an overhead crane moving giant tree trunks around like matchsticks. She has a turban of blue material that also matched our front room curtains – strange headwear! She is also wearing a sack apron. Her nickname was 'Smiler' but in later years she suffered with Alzheimer's. I remember all these ladies' names except one. (Mavis Rigby)

My paternal grandfather George Mundy at his second wedding on 3 September 1913. My grandmother died in March 1912 and a year and a half later my grandfather who lived in Godalming, Surrey, married Sarah Ann Dowling when he was fifty-seven years old and she was forty-seven. The fashions are typical of that post-Edwardian period and were about to change dramatically with the start of the First World War only a year later. (Constance Mundy)

My grandmother Florence Ada Stephenson when she was about eighteen years old, wearing the dress of a young girl in 1900, very different from the fashion of 2000. When I was young I used to stay with my grandma after my grandad died. She used to tell me all about her younger life. The most interesting story was about a lady who lived in West Auckland (where my grandma lived) called Mary Ann Cotton, who killed quite a few people. A programme about her was done by Tyne Tees TV which confirmed what my grandma had told me. (Walter Marshall)

This picture was taken about ten years ago, during a trip to Bath. The old gentleman was looking in dustbins, before I caught the image of him walking past Marks & Spencer. I love the panel of what will be a great image for future generations; Marks & Spencer, who have suffered loss in profits over recent years, have been a household name during most of this gentleman's lifetime. Fierce competition in the fashion industry has contributed to their near collapse. (Wayne Perry)

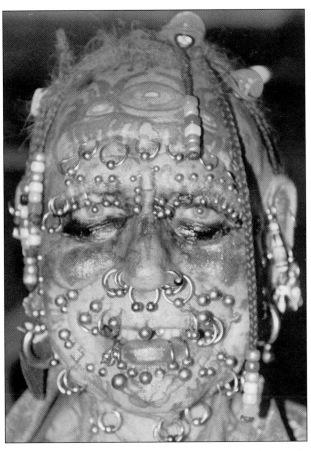

I have always been interested in tattoos, so when I saw this gentleman I asked him if I could take his photo. I think it will be of interest to future generations to see what people did for art and fashion in the year 2000. (Mark Jones)

My grandmother Frances. She and my grandfather William owned a grocery store in the main street of a small village in Co. Tyrone. Their pride and joy was a pony and trap, and it wasn't unusual to see them travel to church on a Sunday in this manner. Note the spectacles, which John Lennon brought back into fashion many years later. (Noreen Dane)

My father-in-law, William Iles, aged sixteen, playing with the other members of his band. How different they are to the 'boy bands' of today and probably those of the future. (Nina Iles, **Winner**)

This photograph of my father with his sister and parents was taken by a street photographer in 1927 at Mablethorpe in Lincolnshire. It reflects the formal attitude of the period: even a day out at the seaside shows a strict code of dress. (Andrew Dunford-Swirles)

My mother aged fifteen with her first serious boyfriend, Roy, on the Palace Pier in Brighton, 1959. Full skirts were in fashion then, and to make them stand out my mother spent hours sewing tiered net petticoats which were then starched. Stiletto shoes were the mode: their heels contained a thread into which could be inserted steel screws for self-repair. With wear, these heels became razor-sharp and left thousands of tiny circles in linoleum and parquet flooring. The cowboy hats were just a fun thing to wear on a seaside day out! (Julie-Anne Bromley)

Me and my fiancé in Bridlington a year before the outbreak of war. We were dressed in the typical fashion of the time, generally with a raincoat at hand. I made my dress myself from 3 yards of good quality cotton material, costing 1s 11d per yard. The white collar was bought ready made. Shoes with the latest ankle strap cost about 5s. My fiancé wore braces, like most men, but with a fashionable narrow tie. Little did we know that in a year we would both be in army uniform. (Irene Monks)

This was taken during a project I was undertaking in the West Midlands in 1986 looking at the African Caribbean community. I had photographed quite a lot of people, old, young, male and female, Rastafarians, mothers and babies, shopkeepers, nurses, etc. It was near the end of the day and a group of young children were playing. I asked if I could photograph them, and they said yes with such ease. A young girl in a red dress and sunglasses made herself visible . . . she posed against a wall – and the picture says it all. (Pogus Caesar, **Runner Up**)

There is a real contrast between the pose of these children, serious faced and wearing formal clothing and a twenty-first century child with sports equipment. Note the sleeves and the waisted and non-waisted clothes, depending on the child's age. (Helen McKeoown)

This photograph is important to me because it is a photograph of my mum as a baby. She is with my grandmother, my great-grandmother, and my great-great-grandmother. It shows how women in three age groups dressed at this time, and also what babies wore. It gives some idea of how people decorated and furnished their homes. (Lucy Dolman, Flint High School, **Secondary School Winner**)

The photograph of these boys was not taken for any particular reason – they just happened to be there! However, the occasion is unique because it illustrates clearly the style of dress prevalent forty years ago. This was long before the days of trainers, t-shirts and baseball caps. This was the era of short trousers, lace-up shoes, wellington boots and pullovers. All these boys are now grown up and have families of their own. (Derek Harding, **Winner**)

This was taken one month before Mr Clarkson retired and his bespoke tailor's shop closed. He'd worked there for fifty-one years and his shop was a wonderful place, with beautifully made clothes in a wood-panelled chest with ornate fittings and mirrors. There was a workroom above the shop and an old stockroom, where this photograph was taken, full of old hat boxes and trousers. The changes in fashions and retail practice have meant that such places are disappearing. (Michael Pearson)

This photograph is special to me because it shows how much my mum loves my sister and me. It reminds me of how she is still supporting us even though we are adults. The flats where the photograph was taken were knocked down last year. They were where I was born and where my nan lived until she died. This photograph is also important to show the fashions of the 1970s. I'm OK but what on earth are my mum and sister wearing? (Christine McBurney)

On the south coast, possibly Hastings, *c.* 1930. It shows my mother and father before they were married, her older sister (left) and her son. Note that smart dress was even required on the beach in those days. (Trevor Smithers)

Right: My mother on the right, with a friend. I wish I knew where the photo was taken, in a studio in London perhaps? It shows the fashion of that era. In later life she became very anti-cruelty, and she would not have worn that fur stole or whatever it is. To me the style is typical 1920s and I like the photo very much. I hope it will be of interest. (Frank Gregory, **Winner**)

Sitting pretty by the sea at Blackpool, my grandmother Flora Clutton Cooper and her cousin May, 16 July 1927. How fashions and attitudes have changed – who would sit on the beach today dressed in their day frock with hat, not to mention the stockings and smart shoes they would also have worn? On a personal note, earlier in the day my grandmother, a young widow with two small children, had remarried at Basford register office, Nottinghamshire, and found happiness again. (Karen Parsons)

This is a picture of my great-great-great-aunt Elizabeth from my mother's side of the family. She was born at 3 White Horse Lane, Stepney, London, on 24 February 1839. This picture was taken about 1860 so she was twenty-one years old. She married a man from New Zealand called Mr Denton and they lived outside Blackpool in Lancashire. This shows the fine clothes of the nineteenth century that ladies wore. (Katie Eynon, Highfield School, **Primary School Winner**)

My grandma's wedding was just after the war and that is why she is not wearing a wedding dress. I like it because it shows me what she looked like when she was young, and what clothes were like just after the war. It is also nice because I can see how much she has changed since then. (Rosie Bruce, Hotspur Primary School)

The annual summer holiday when most factories closed for two weeks was anticipated all year and you would save to buy new clothes. The dress shows the 1930s shape, with a belted waist and long, slim skirt, mid-calf length. Hats were worn at an angle with short permed hair. The pearl necklace was a fashionable accessory as Chanel made costume jewellery popular. (Beverley Reynolds, **Runner Up**)

I think this photograph will be useful in a hundred years because it will look at the fashion of women two centuries before. This photograph of my great-grandmother was taken in the year 1900. Her name was Esmerelda Rose, and in this picture she was eighteen years old! (Sarah Beames, Griffithstown Junior School)

A family wedding. The picture is of personal value to me because on the left-hand side the two men are my great-grandad and my great-great granddad and great-great-grandma in front. It will be of interest to future generations because it shows the costumes worn for a wedding at the beginning of the twentieth century. (Luke Iremonger, Gayton Junior School)

This photograph was taken at a friend's wedding in Glasgow in April 1970. I think it reflects the fashion of the day – the midi-length skirt (after the mini-skirts of the late '60s), floral long jacket, clumpy shoes and bag to contrast with the delicate hat and floral print. Despite the formal occasion, it reflects our interest in fashion and how fashion can remind us of a time and place from the past. It was also a joyful time. (Sylvie Duncan, **Runner Up**)

This photo of my aunt and her friend shows an indispensable fashion accessory of the 1950s, the plastic mac! It could be folded up and easily carried around, an example of how the invention of new materials affects everyday life. The photo also shows the typical shawl collar and full skirt fashionable in the 1950s. The nylon stockings, which had then become easily available, and the handbags over the arm, are also typical of the decade. (Beverley Reynolds)

This is a photo taken in 1969 of my uncle Ken's christening. It is of personal value to me because the picture contains a lot of the older generations of my family, including my mum – the smallest girl near the front. It will be of interest to future generations as it shows that in the '60s ladies wore hats and gloves to church and all the coats had collars. It also shows a range of clothing over a variety of ages in the 'Swinging Sixties'. (Mark Pomroy, Gayton Junior School)

I think this photograph is special because it is me on holiday when I was two years old. I am wearing my favourite swimming costume. People will like to look at this photo in the future to see what children wore at the seaside. (Sasha Joy Gapaul, Highcliffe Primary School)

We call this photo 'two weddings and a funeral'. 1932 was a significant year in our family history as Lily's sister was married on Easter Sunday, her mother died a few weeks later and finally Lily married on Boxing Day. Lily's two sisters seated on the right are both wearing grey outfits as a sign of mourning. The fashions are typical of the late 1920s/early 1930s, with the cloche hats and the slim silhouette of the bride's dress. My aunt remembers her bridesmaid dress was all white with pink embroidery round the neck. (Kenneth Reynolds)

My maternal great-grandparents, William and Jemima Sanderson. He was a wagonwright at a colliery in County Durham. I think it is a fascinating insight into how my great-grandparents looked and dressed and will be of interest to my children and grandchildren. When she married Jemima apparently could not write, and signed her marriage certificate with an X. William, judging by the nature of his trade, earned his living by the skill of his hands. (Janet Stevenson, **Runner Up**)

My grandmother in her Girl Guide uniform. She is thirteen years old in the photograph and the year is 1928. I think people will be surprised to see how different the uniform was, and yet how the movement has lasted all these years. (Sarah Dicks)

This photograph of my great-grandma's wedding took place in Sydney, Australia, on 10 October 1910. She chose Australia because a lot of her relations lived there. This photograph is important to my family because it pictures the marriage of my great-grandparents. The gentleman on the bride's right is my great-grandad and the old lady sitting down to the left of the photograph is my great-great-great-aunt May. This photograph will be useful to historians for it shows the fashionable things to wear to a wedding in the early twentieth century. (Fiona McClean)

My mother's godmother with Queen Mary. It was taken in 1936 outside Althorp in Northamptonshire, the home of Lord and Lady Spencer. My mother's godmother was Lady Spencer; she is on the far left of the picture and was lady-in-waiting to Queen Elizabeth the Queen Mother. This is of personal value because it includes my mother's godmother, and is of historical value because it shows Queen Mary, and what people wore in those days. The boy with the dog and the man behind him are the father and grandfather of Diana, Princess of Wales. (Robert Crowter-Jones, Hazel Down School)

This photograph is of my great-grandmother and her two grandchildren. The boy and girl in the photograph are now sixty-nine years old and sixty-five years old. The lady is wearing an apron over her dress, and the baby boy she is holding is wearing a dress. The girl is wearing a skirt, which is probably handmade, and a knitted jumper. Her hair was cut by her father. The photo shows how people dressed around the early 1930s. (Richard Kincaid, New Buildings Primary School)

My grandparents on their wedding day, August 1964. The wedding took place at St Peter's Church, Cockett, Swansea. Clothes, fashions and hairstyles have all changed. I like the photo because it shows me how my grandparents looked nearly thirty-seven years ago: my grandpa has lost a lot of hair and my nan's has turned grey. I will treasure the photo because as time passes it will never alter. In a hundred years time photography will be quite different. (Emma Colwill, St Josephs Junior School)

I think that this captures the fashions of the 1960s, right from the white boots to the short leather skirt. My nan used to ride around in the limos. She was so popular in her time that she even had her picture in the paper. (Alex Cheshire, Sholing Girls School)

My uncles in September 1975. I think the photo represents the fashions and trends in that decade. One fashion was flared trousers, which tended to be long and baggy. The clothes were also bold and beautiful. Although it is not effectively shown in the black and white photo, shorts and other normally plain items were colourful and had striking patterns. The way people look can be influenced by famous people. For example, the Beatles influenced men to grow their hair long. Will these fashions be worn in the future? (Andrew Pellegrini, St Paul's Catholic College, **Secondary School Winner**)

My father as a boy of thirteen with his brother and family. The stiff pose shows how much fashions, holidays and childhood have changed. Even though they are on holiday my father and his brother are wearing suits. Clothes were still on ration after the war. The girl standing up has a deformed arm. This was because it wasn't set when broken. This was before the days of the NHS, and shows how much medical science has changed. (Hannah Tugby, Wyggeston and Queen Elizabeth College)

This is a picture of Rose and Harold Humphrey getting married in 1947. The bride is wearing very fashionable clothes for the time. Her shoes are quite high and her hat expensive – definitely not the type of clothes they would have worn every day. Harold is wearing a suit that is very much like something you might see today at a wedding, but it is obvious that women's fashions have changed a lot since then. (Honor Hewett, St Paul's Catholic College, **Secondary School Winner**)

This photograph is of my great-great-nan, Lydia. She was a milliner (which means she made hats) in Southampton. The photo shows one of her designs. Her job was important because ladies wouldn't go out without wearing a hat! My mum, nanny and two aunties have carried on the tradition. They run a shop called Lydia's Hats, where ladies can hire hats for special occasions. At Royal Ascot my family wears their special hat designs. This photo might be of historical value because people will be able to see what sort of clothing used to be worn in 1886. (Suzie Marsh, Sholing Girls School)

This is a photo of my mum taken when she was five years old. The picture reflects the fashions of the 1960s, showing us the way people dressed. In the picture she is wearing one of her best outfits because it was the first time she went to church without going to the Sunday School. I think the picture would be of interest to future generations as you no longer see children dressed this way. It also shows that church was an important part of life which isn't so important now. (Nicole Andrews, Wyggeston & Queen Elizabeth College, **Secondary School Winner**)

This is my mother when she was about eleven or twelve years old. She is the one in the middle. Her name is Jan. It shows what the fashion was like in the late '60s and early '70s.
(Kathryn Hemming, Ringwood School, **Secondary School Winner**)

This picture was taken on 31 January 1959 at Wood Green Register Office in London. The occasion was my grandmother and grandfather's wedding day. The picture is of my grandmother Pamela Ali, on the right, in the middle her mother, my great-grandmother Barbara Barnes, and on the left my grandma's twin sister Jean Barnes. As you can see from the picture the shoes which they are wearing are stiletto shoes, which are still worn today. The skirts in those days were worn below the knee. My grandma and grandpa celebrated their fortieth wedding anniversary last year.
(Roxanne Olivia Painter, Stanborough School, **Secondary School Winner**)

town & country

My great-grandfather, Robert Holmes, in 1938. He was a bus driver.
He drove for forty-five years, including during two world wars. This
must have been dangerous work. For fifteen years he provided a vital
link between country areas and isolated farms centred on Eaglesham
and the city of Glasgow. Buses were essential in those days as few
people had cars. He loved his job, but there is an added sadness
because he died behind the wheel of his bus in 1960. (Gemma Parks,
Duncanrig Secondary School, **Secondary School Winner**)

This photograph shows what transport was available in the 1920s. I think it will be important to show future generations that not all transport is cars, trains and aeroplanes. The horses are used to pull carts and for other jobs on farms, for example ploughing. One of the people in the carriage would have driven. The two people are my great-great aunts. This photo was taken in Marden, Kent. (Hannah Ward, Ashford School, **Secondary School Winner**)

This is a photo of my grandfather with his first car. He was the first person in the village to have one. People were jealous of this, but being the kind man he was, he took people for rides up and down the village. (Amy Jones, Aberdare Girls' School, **Secondary School Winner**)

This picture of some of my dad's uncles and aunts was taken in the summer of 1950, just before my dad's christening. The man standing at the back on the right is my great-great-uncle Bert. My dad was named after Uncle Bert's son Ron, who had been killed at the Battle of Arnhem in Holland during the Second World War. They were on a special day out to Brighton and all the family went in a coach. This shows family history and the history of the last century, which I find fascinating. (Joanna Skillett, Coopers Company & Coborn School)

This photo shows my great-grandfather. He lived and grew up here, in St Ives, Cornwall. He was on leave from the navy, and helping the other men to bring the day's fish in. The fish being thrown is a skate. It tells a lot about how things in St Ives have changed since the 1920s. The horse and cart has been replaced by motor vehicles and the fishing boats by more modern and flashy ones. I think this photo shows a very important part of St Ives' history, and can be used to show what this town and its way of life used to be like. (Holly Lovegrove, Cockermouth School, **Secondary School Winner**)

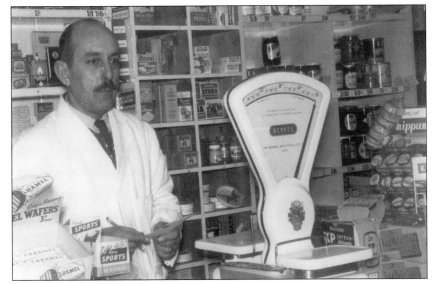

My grandfather in the late 1950s. He is behind the counter of his corner shop in Exeter, Devon. People used to shop in here daily, as this was before supermarkets. He sold groceries and fruit and vegetables. Sweets and biscuits were sold loose, not in packaging. Some products look the same today as they did then. The shop opened 8.30 a.m. to 6.00 p.m. Monday to Saturday and closed early at 1.00 p.m. on Wednesday. My dad used to help stack the shelves, and when he was older he would serve behind the counter to earn his pocket money. (Sarah Cocks, Danes Hill School, **Primary School Winner**)

This is a picture of my great-grandfather, who was a doctor. His name was William Taylour Doyle Allen, and in this picture he is sitting on a bed in the children's ward of the Brownlow Hill Hospital in Liverpool where he was the Resident Medical Officer. This picture was taken in about 1903 and shows what hospitals were like and what the nurses wore then. My grandfather still has the watch that his father is wearing in this picture. (Charlotte Eynon, Highfield School, **Primary School Winner**)

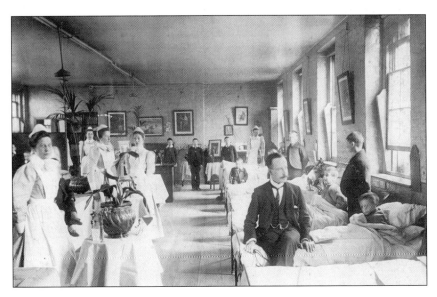

This picture shows my great-grandad Tom Gunn (left), who was skipper of the *Smiling Morn*, with a crew member. They had just caught a giant halibut. It weighed 12 stone and was more than 6 feet long. This picture is important because it shows people the big halibut that you could catch in the North Sea in 1961. (Steffi Niwa, Hillhead Primary School, **Primary School Winner**)

A Preston North End team with my grandad and Sir Tom Finney: they were both members of the same team. As you can see the football kits were a lot plainer and simpler than the ones today. Also the boots were a lot heavier, while the ball's outer case was made of leather and the inside of the ball was a bladder. This photo was taken on Preston North End's ground. My grandad was playing in a cup game in 1938 just before the war; then he fought and served four years abroad. This photo is of historic value to my grandad because it reminds him of playing football in his younger days, before the Second World War broke out and his life was changed. (Caroline Fletcher, Brownedge St Mary's, **Secondary School Winner**)

My mum sitting on a motorbike and sidecar outside the house, 1959. Where she used to live in the late 1950s, in the part of London shown in the picture, living conditions for some people were fairly cramped. The house where my mum lived was occupied by her parents, grandparents, a few of her aunties, a dog and a cat. There was no bathroom and one outside toilet. Coal fires heated the house and the laundry was done by hand in the scullery. How day-to-day life has changed over the past forty years. (Grace Leborgne, Coopers Company & Coborn School)

This photo depicts a typical family day out in the 1930s. The old-fashioned swimsuits the men are wearing and the women's coats and even furs are very strange, I think. They are in front of a beach hut, and the whole scene is very different from a modern trip to the beach. I think it's a great family photo, showing the generations of my family from my great-great-great-auntie to my grandfather. (Kate Ainsley, Ivybridge Community College)

My great-grandad George Manson (second left) on the steam drifter *Brae Flett* in Wick Harbour, c. 1925. The boat would have fished for herring. It was owned by the Flett family. The two ladies may have been the captain's and engineer's wives. This is an important picture because it shows how big a crew worked on a steam drifter. It also shows how busy the harbour is. Boats came to Wick from all over Scotland. The two in the background are from Buckie. It is also interesting to see the clothes the fishermen wore; they all have leather boots. (Roddy Mackay, Hillhead Primary School, **Primary School Winner**)

My brother on my dad's boat *Stratdonah*. He is laughing because of all the fish around him. This is an important picture because it shows how fish look when they are caught in the North Sea. In the future fish may not be caught like this. (David Macadie, Hillhead Primary School, **Primary School Winner**)

I chose this picture because I thought that my dad had not won anything in his life, but now I know he has! He won a father and son competition. They don't look the same now. My grandad and dad came first. My dad has not changed, but now my grandad has white hair and false teeth! This was taken on 1 July 1967. It came with a free trip to Butlin's. (Anna Hardy, Humberston School)

On 5 September each year the female members of my nan's family went hop picking to Bishop Frome, Herefordshire. The children were kept away from school, although they knew there'd be a fine from truancy officers. Their home was a barn and they slept on bales of hay. There was a lot of community spirit and cooking was done outdoors. The standard diet was stew and apple dumplings. Everyone picked the hops. These were weighed daily and entered into a tally book. Everyone was then paid at the end of the month. My great-nan was paid £52, a lot of money! (Jemma Tivendale, The Kingswinford School, **Secondary School Winner**)

These are my ancestors on my mother's side in 1894. The lady standing is my great-great-grandmother. The older lady is the baby's grandmother, my great-great-great-grandmother. The cottage was situated at the foot of Scrabo Hill in Newtownards, County Down. They would have had no running water, no electricity and no sewerage system. Cooking would have been done over an open fire. This photograph will be useful for future generations because it shows them how things used to be, and how many technical advances there have been over the century. (Andrew Neil Carlisle, Royal Belfast Academic Institution, **Secondary School Winner**)

My grandmother Dorothy McEvoy, who was Ford Aero Engines' top female driver, was going in for the Monte Carlo rally car race with Amy Johnson, who was the first woman to fly solo, and Sir Malcolm Campbell, who broke the land speed record. Tragically during the war, in 1941, Amy Johnson was shot down while flying an allied plane. My grandmother changed to chauffeuring people such as King Olaf of Norway and the Duke of Kent while working for Ford Aero Engines. (Emma Russell, Ringwood Comprehensive School, **Secondary School Winner**)

This photo means a lot to me and my friends because it shows friendship. We took part in the Reading mini marathon and ran for the Imperial Cancer Research Fund. We chose to run for this charity because my dad died of cancer just before Christmas and he would have liked me and my friends to run for other people in his position. Me and my friends found out about this marathon from a presentation at school and thought it would be a good opportunity to run in memory of my dad. My dad would have been very proud of me. (Daniel Hall, St Crispin's School)

This is my dad when he worked down the coal mines. He is the man furthest to the right. This was one of Cannock Chase's biggest mines, but no it longer exists. There were over two hundred mines in Cannock many years ago, and when the photo was taken in 1987 there were only three. Also in the picture is Sir Robert Haslam, the chairman of the Coal Board. My dad was an engineer; he fixed the machines that dug out the coal. This industry is now dead. (Laura Graham, St Dominic's Priory School)

This photograph of a hulk was taken in 1902 on the Niger. White traders in Nigeria were badly affected by malaria. They thought that if they lived away from the land, in old sailing ships, they would be immune to the disease: they didn't realise that mosquitoes carried it. So they stripped old sailing ships, put a roof on them, and lived and traded from them. Unfortunately stagnant water was in the hulls of these ships, so the mosquitoes bred quickly, worsening the malaria. It is relevant to me because my grandfather traded in Nigeria and raised his family there. (Alexandra Du Denny, St Paul's Catholic College, **Secondary School Winner**)

My grandpa, Peter Jennings Stuttard, was born in Todmorden, Yorkshire, in 1921. When he was a little boy he didn't walk or drive a car to church, but would ride every Sunday on the back of Jinny, the donkey, with his sister Judy, in a special wicker basket. In the photograph my grandpa's great-aunt Minnie is holding the donkey. This photograph shows a way of life already gone. In another hundred years I'm sure it will be even more interesting for people to look at. It's like looking through a window into history. (Jessica McSlog, St Margaret's School)

Mr Mervyn Webber and his brother have both worked as blacksmiths at this smithy since they were young men. Both are now in their eighties. They work regularly every day using traditional methods. As a keen photographer and a former chartered engineer I was keen to take photographs of them at work. Traditional blacksmithing is a dying skill. Very few young men want to follow the trade and of course there is reduced demand for this type of work. Both the Mr Webbers take great pride in their work and enjoy it. (John Burles)

The year is 1938, the last summer before the Second World War, and my grandparents are on holiday with their eldest daughter. My grandfather Archibald Boulton Thomson is ready for action on the beach at Paignton. With his airbed, newspaper and towel around his shoulders (to stop sunburn) he looks prepared for anything and is determined to enjoy himself. The family had previously gone to France for their holidays. My grandfather was a fluent French speaker and during the war he was posted to France to work undercover with the Resistance. (Katharine McKinnon, **Winner**)

This photograph is an inspiration to me. It shows that where there is a will there is a way! My hope is that it will inspire future generations to achieve what they want to, even if they do not have sophisticated equipment and facilities. This photograph shows that if you have determination you can achieve, without money, correct kit, high-tech training facilities or good weather! So do not make excuses – just go and do it. (Jennifer Fox-Johnson, **Runner Up**)

A steam locomotive-hauled excursion express arriving at Blackpool Central Station from Stockport, June 1962. The footplate crew, driver Frank Moss and fireman Ron Prince, would have worked hard during the journey, using 4½ tons of coal and 4,500 gallons of water to maintain 250 lb of steam pressure to enable the train to run at speeds of up to 95 mph. The 1950s and 1960s were the real heyday for steam locomotive-hauled excursion trains. (Ronald Prince, **Runner Up**)

I was walking through the older parts of Bristol one Sunday morning looking for old buildings to photograph. This young boy was running around the play area with such enthusiasm that I had to take his photograph. The murals are by local amateurs, and in the future will be overtaken by formal modern façades. The picture expresses youthful optimism against a decaying background. (Raymond Kennedy, **Runner Up**)

Dinner for two. In earlier years it would have provided rabbit stew for the family of nine. Grandfather lived alone in the house in the forest, surviving wartime near misses from crashing aeroplanes, forest fires from incendiary bombs, isolated by an unexploded land mine and an almost direct hit nearly demolishing house and family. But the 400 year old beams and joists held firm. Grandfather died and the house became derelict, bereft of roof tiles and windows. Now the woodlands have been restored, and happy children are again heard playing in the forest. (Tilly Campbell)

These are old bowser pumps which my father had when he first started in business. You had to pump the petrol by hand. As you can see petrol was 1s ½d a gallon for Dingle and 1s for Clarion. His garage was on the A540 Chester Road and is still there today, only nothing like this photo at all. (Rosemary Abraham)

A happy group of people stopping for refreshments while haymaking. It is not known who they are: the photo was taken from a glass plate left to me by an old gentleman whose father was a shepherd, and who may well be in the picture. Probably the lady and girl have brought food to the men. It shows hard-working men happy (I think) in their pursuits. Note the men's hobnail boots and women's Edwardian fashions. The men are very swarthy with outdoor work. (Jean Moore, **Runner Up**)

This picture was taken in the 1940s by my father. It shows my mother standing in front of a 1934 Singer coupé. Both my mother and the car are things of beauty. The car still remains in my dad's garage and is in mint condition, and will remain so to prove to future generations that they do not make this sort of thing today. (Michael Hawkins, **Royal British Legion Winner**)

This photograph represents five generations, from Alexander MacKinnon aged 101 to the baby of a few months old. Alexander MacKinnon is my great-great-great-grandfather who was born in 1799 and died aged 104 – and had the distinction of living in three centuries. The achievements of Nelson and Wellington took place during his boyhood. His forefathers from Mull and Skye fought alongside Bonnie Prince Charlie; one was honoured by Napoleon Bonaparte and another was a close friend of Samuel Johnson (the great Englishman). He is buried at the parish churchyard in Ballintoy with the headstone inscription 'audentes fortuna juvat' – 'fortune favours the brave'.
(Trevor Moffet)

This photo conveys the atmosphere and characteristic appearance of sheep farmers in the Yorkshire Dales at an auction. The auctioneer is calling the prices in a rapid monotone, awaiting a cursory nod of acceptance from one of the flat-capped farmers. The setting is unique and representative of the period. (Raymond Kennedy)

I took this photograph of New Brighton in 1950. Most of the people probably came over the Mersey from Liverpool for a day out at the seaside. Today it would be a totally different scene as the pier has disappeared and so have the people to sunnier climes, where they don't have to roll up their trousers to go for a paddle.
(Peter Moore)

This is Kevin Keegan, who was at the time manager of Newcastle United, and two United players at Maiden Castle, Durham, the area they used for training at that time. Soon after the photograph was taken Keegan resigned as manager of Newcastle. I often watched the players train as Keegan encouraged the public to watch, and I noticed how he appeared to be preoccupied. If there was a defining moment when he made up his mind to leave Newcastle this may very well have been that moment, in which case this may have been when England's chances of winning the next World Cup or even of performing well in Euro 2000 took a turn for the better. (John Burles)

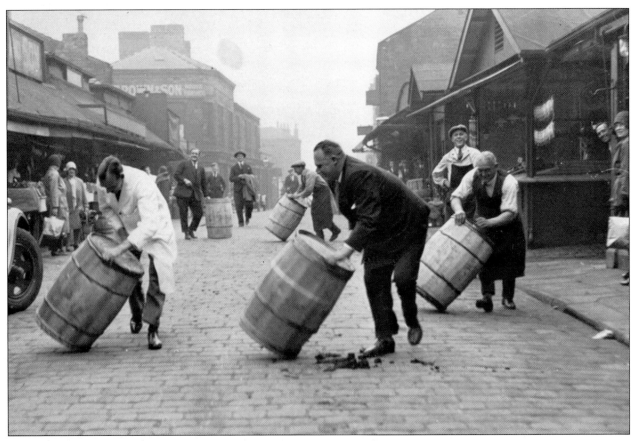

The photograph was taken at Keighley Market by G.A. Shore, c. 1929. The cloche hats worn by the ladies are very much of the period. My uncle Harry Hoyle and my father Albert Hoyle (greengrocers) are in the front of the picture. The traders worked long hours but sometimes, on a quiet Monday morning, they could have a bit of fun. Keighley Market, which was granted a charter in 1305, is now entirely under cover, and the days of rolling barrels along the cobbles among the horse dung will not be seen again. (Nesta Hoyle, **Overall Winner**)

The Houston family's smallholding was farmed without tractor or the use of electricity throughout the whole of the twentieth century. If farm machinery could not be operated by hand or by horse it was not used. I took this photograph of Alex Houston with his horse and machine busy raking hay, which was later built by hand into stacks. A rare sight in the UK during the 1980s and now a treasured memory, this sight is now history as Alex Houston died during 1997 and the farm is no longer worked by the family. (Stewart Wilson)

There are currently between 9,300 and 10,000 gypsies and travellers in the United Kingdom. The family is a large, tightly knit, cohesive group both socially and economically. I photographed this gypsy at the Cotswold town of Stow-on-the-Wold in May 1990. The field and lane were filled with parked vardos, waggons and stalls selling china, chromeware, clothes, antiques and horse-tack. Horse fairs and races around the country provide an opportunity for a celebration of traveller culture, and although they are now just a shadow of their former glory, they still have great atmosphere, energy and life. (Ruhi Farmer)

Before its removal, in 1960, to Harford on the outskirts of the city, the Norwich Livestock Market was held on the hill in the shadow of the castle. Many of the cattle came from the country by train, completing their journey from the station by being herded through the city's streets. On one such occasion (in 1937) three of them escaped, stampeding through several thoroughfares until being corralled in the Sir Thomas Browne Memorial Garden. The photograph serves a dual purpose as it also shows the garden before its destruction in 1972 to be replaced by stone paving. (George Plunkett)

This is my grandfather (dadcu in Welsh). On the back of the bike is his sister Kate; they were two of fourteen children. Kate was 100 on 14 April 2000. I think it's of interest because grandad had motorbikes, my father Richard had motorbikes, I ride motorbikes and so does my son Leigh – so we have four generations of bikers! This bike sadly burned when an outside shed caught fire, but I am sure I have seen EJ 409 on a Mercedes locally! Kate married Fred Sauvey from Jersey. He was chief electrician in Westminster Abbey. (Mariann Denyer)

Packing saggars in a bottle oven. An oven held hundreds of saggars all fitted with ware, so careful and skilful work was essential. If any saggar should fall it would mean the loss of thousands of pounds and time. The pottery workers called the stepladders in the photo the 'little hoss' and 'the big hoss' – hoss being the Potteries dialect for horse. (Donald Morris)

My brother-in-law, Edmund Thorpe, is the last in his family to farm the bleak moorland that encircles his rambling farmhouse on the Lancashire Pennines. At the beginning of the new century, hill farming is no longer able to provide a living for these hard-working people and soon it will be a thing of the past. This photograph depicts a shy, solitary man, but one who is able to face adversity with a dry sense of humour and a smile. (Robin Sharples, **Runner Up**)

This photo was taken of my father's first scrap metal shop at Notting Hill in about 1938. It shows children having fun on the streets of Notting Hill Dale with the sound of a barrel organ. When I look at this picture I see many things: although times were hard the children look well fed and clothed, but their lives would change in a year or two. Instead of the noise from a barrel organ they would hear the sound of bombs, although the East End of London was bombed more than the west during the Second World War. (Raymond Stentaford)

In 1908 a local landowner blocked an ancient right of way across the golf-course at Seathorne (Winthorpe), Skegness. This denied local workers access to farmland and sea. Here my grandfather, Samuel Moody, is seen cutting the barbed wire to allow access once more. He fought and won a legal battle on behalf of the workers against the landowner and the right of way remains in use to this day. The case was heard at Lincoln Assizes, and the judge was Charles Dickens' son. (Mary Peet, **Winner**)

The photograph was taken on Westwood Farm, St Ives, Cambridgeshire, by Miss Oliver, who was on holiday there in 1933. It shows a local character, 'Baggy Reynolds', a farmhand working there. Milking was done by hand, and if fine in the open. The farm has now gone and the site is a housing estate and recreation centre. I managed to date the photograph because in 1937 Baggy Reynolds went to work on the roads. The negative is part of a collection given to me. (Allan Mott)

This is a picture of my dad (kneeling) and his mates at the end of a shift on the coalface in 1998. He spent twenty-five years down the pit at Silverdale Colliery. He was so proud of being a miner, always talking about the comradeship and trust of his mates in dangerous conditions. I can remember him having a bad accident and going to see him in hospital but his favourite saying was 'through pitfalls some good some bad I'm proud to be a mining lad'. Three weeks after the photo was taken the pit shut so ending mining in Staffordshire forever. (Andrew Leese, **Sky Digital Winner**)

This is a picture of my father, David McCracken (on the right) and his pal, David Robertson or as I liked to call them, the two Davys. It was taken in their favourite haunt, the local working men's club. They were both typical working-class men of their time – as can be seen from the beer, tabs and flat caps. My father always had his flat cap on, only removing it for bed, and his friend always seemed to have a tab hanging from his mouth. My father is gone now, but this photo shows him at his happiest at the club. (David McCracken)

Remember the corner shop? Before the days of the big supermarket we all purchased from the local shop. It seems this shop, seen here in 1959, took account of the Potteries atmosphere for in the window we see Oxydol, Daz, Tide, Fairy and Ajax! There are also Hacks and Victory Vs, both sweets for sore throats. (Donald Morris)

The photograph is of one of the last surviving corner stores. I do not know if it is still there, as the photo is twenty-three years old. As you can see all items are on display. It shows how corner shops survived even to 1977. It also shows us celebrating the Queen's Silver Jubilee; we later went on to have a street party. This was brilliant as lots of us lived in blocks of flats. The community spirit was terrific. Castle Vale, Farnborough, has changed a lot. (Josephine Brunt)

This is my grandmother Blanche, bottom right. She worked for Plymouth Breweries from the age of fourteen until the beginning of the war. Blanche's hands were badly scarred from injuries sustained from exploding bottles, but she was never bitter. In fact she was very proud to have worked for Plymouth Brewery which is now historically important as it no longer exists. Now there is only the Plymouth gin distillery which Blanche was born almost next door to. During the war she worked serving drinks in the NAAFI. One funny thing is that Blanche hated people who got drunk. (Elizabeth Beavis)

The photograph is of personal value because Lyme Regis provides a traditional bucket and spade family holiday: my husband came as a child, as did our daughter, as will our granddaughter. Live entertainment has a feeling of continuity down the generations. Lyme, a fishing harbour, has found fame in the film *The French Lieutenant's Woman*, which features its unique sea defence, the Cobb. It can be seen in old photographs and is unchanged today. Punch and Judy shows should also be captured for posterity: they may one day no longer exist. (Patricia Stokes)

This is my grandfather sitting perched 'up top' in his cab. The picture was taken at the turn of the last century. His nephews helped with the nightly feeding and stabling of the horse and with the maintenance of the cab. The blanket wrapped around his legs indicates it was a cold way to earn a living. His children loved to see him take 'fares' to the races – everyone dressed up and hats were worn. Pollution would not have featured in any conversation. He was happy in his work. He died, alas, young and I never knew him. (Shirley Oxenbury)

The bus inspector was my father, Micky Charles. He was a sergeant in the RAF during the Second World War and joined London Transport after demobilisation in 1946, retiring in 1983. As his father before him he was a good, hard-working man possessing a rare sense of humour. Proud of his English heritage and traditions, a firm believer in family values and education, at times an outspoken critic of hypocrisy and oppression, he never won any medals or gained public recognition but, by his example, left his family a lasting legacy. (Pamela Hill, **Runner Up**)

I found this photograph of my wife Jean's grandfather in a box of old mementoes. On the back of one postcard he has asked the photographer to include a letter from King Edward VII – dated 6 May 1903. It reads: 'Sir, I have had the honour of submitting your letter to the King, and I am commanded, in reply, to thank you for the copy of the photograph which you have sent him of a statue of Queen Victoria, which was presented to Newcastle upon Tyne by Sir William Stephenson. I am your obedient servant.' I presume that the statue is still there although I'm not sure if there's still the same level of pride in the royal family! (Jean & Bill Hunt)

This shows the degree of atmospheric pollution in Glasgow in 1959. In addition to the heavy industry of that time much of the smoke came from burning coal for domestic heating throughout the city, even in the well-to-do areas, which did not have central heating with gas or electricity for some years. Although the Clean Air Act came into force in 1956, coal burning continued for a long time. All the very poor-quality elderly tenements shown here were demolished by the '70s. That this picture was taken on a sunny day is shown by the shadows seen on the near roofs, cast by the chimney-stacks. (Michael Smith)

Harold Wright (master thatcher) making hazel spars to keep the thatch in place at the ridge of the roof. Each year in September at Compton in Somerset he opens his home to the public in order to raise money for cancer research. I think this is an important image as it shows a continuing traditional activity. His sons continue the family business and he still makes the spars. (Caroline Bagias)

Left: My grandad in a rickshaw being carried by a Zulu, Durban, South Africa, 1943. It cost sixpence a mile. This picture is important to history because the transport used in South Africa in the war will have changed now and transport isn't man powered. (Polly Mason, Taverham Middle School)

This is interesting for me because it shows me how wealthy people travelled before the Second World War although many of them had motor cars. This picture was taken in India in 1938 just before the war. The lady driving is my friend's mother-in-law and she is still alive. The man who is at the back is the servant. His job was to care for the horses and their tack. The carriage and horses are called a carriage and pair, because there are two horses. (Patricia Pacheco, Hillside Junior School)

My grandfather, aged just fourteen, in July 1914 following his first day's work after leaving school. He worked underground at Cwmaman Colliery in South Wales for twelve hours each day, six days a week, starting work at 6.00 a.m. His duties were mainly opening and closing the ventilation doors as the horse-drawn trams containing coal passed by on their way to the pit bottom. These doors were very important as they controlled the flow of fresh air within the coal mine. Accidents to new boy miners underground were frequent, sometimes fatal, but my grandfather survived unscathed (Glyn Picton, **Overall Winner**)

In June 1955 we spent a wonderful week in Blackpool, aged eighteen, our first holiday unescorted by parents. The photograph taken on the Golden Mile sitting astride a Norton motorcycle shows that fashions have not changed much with our shorts, pedal pushers and caps. The town was crowded, the weather glorious. We spent most afternoons at the busy outdoor swimming pool or funfair, returning to the boarding house for evening meal followed by dancing in the Winter Gardens, which was packed to capacity. (Pauline Pascoe)

The annual Whit Friday walk around Mossley in Ashton-Under-Lyne. On the same day in the evening there are the brass band contests where over fifty bands compete for the Best of Brass title of Tameside. Not many towns now have the Whit Week walks but Mossley in Tameside still has them year after year. The photo was taken where all the processions start, at the Market Ground. They move along the streets of Mossley, through Micklehurst and back. The Mossley Whit Walk is always a wonderful display of Christian unity and this year saw more crowds than ever before because of the wonderful weather. (Jean Ann Cain)

The village mummers tradition, which began in pagan times and has almost died out, was the forerunner of modern theatre. The theme of their presentation was the battle between good and evil and renewal or rebirth from death. Their pageants took place at the winter solstice or Christmas in the Christian era. My grandfather's group of mummers included himself as the devil, his brother as a soldier who slays him, a doctor to revive the devil, the king to administer justice and two comic characters, a clown and an old mother figure to chastise the group. (Gerald Martin)

The postwar rationing period of the late 1940s was the peak era for the exodus of immigrants from the UK to Australia. I was five years old and just remember the emotional scenes at the railway station in Kilwenning, Scotland, when scores of friends and neighbours came to wave us off to Liverpool. We sailed on the MV *Georgic* with around 2,000 other emigrants (one of whom my sister Mary married). The photo was taken on arrival in Sydney, and was featured on the front page of the *Sydney Sun*, as we were the largest family ever to emigrate from Scotland. Although we didn't settle there, it is still remembered as a great experience. (Andrew Thompson)

Hungerford belfry, Berkshire, on 29 November 1980. The eight people in the picture had just rung the first ever long length peal on church bells by an all-female band. It took five hours thirty-two minutes to complete. My mum is at the front of the picture on the right-hand side. Church bell ringing started many centuries ago but has really taken off in the past hundred years because travel has become much easier. I have just started bell ringing and I am the eighth member in my family to do so. (Heather Forster, Laleham C of E School)

'Purveyor of horse flesh', as it is says on the barrow. I think people in the future will find it interesting to see how they used to sell horse meat as it all comes in tins now. I am not sure where the photo was taken. My grandfather had a horse cab and knacker's yard in Tottenham Court Road. The photo was taken by W.H. Johnson, Green Street. The only Green Street I know is in Plaistow, London. I think the photo was taken in about 1912. The man on the right of the photo is Alfred Plumley, who was killed in the First World War. (Robert Plumley, **Winner**)

This photograph was taken in 1994 when the Round Britain cycle race was held. This was the leg through Portsmouth, Hampshire. Most roads were closed to traffic and crowds filled the roadsides to cheer the riders on. I was at the back of the crowd, so I held up a small mirror and then focused on the mirror. This photograph was the result. I was quite pleased, as I had to walk 2 miles from my parked vehicle to get to the spot, only to find I was at the rear. (Richard Cooke)

This is a photograph of me holding a large cod on the deck of my trawler in the Irish Sea thirty years ago. In those days fish were still plentiful and our way of life uncomplicated, with no EC rules, regulations, form filling and certainly no quotas. This season for the first time ever a large section of the Irish Sea was closed off for three months to belatedly help diminishing cod stocks. Fishermen received no compensation and hardship was experienced. Now to make a living wage they have to put to sea in even worse weather conditions than before. (Norman Pascoe)

This is a photo of my grandparents, Lou and Violet Holttum, in 1958, at St Nicholas Hospital in Plumstead, London (now a housing estate). My grandmother was in an isolation ward, because of a lump that appeared on her face. She is practising what she preached – that 'a glass of stout helped cure all illnesses'. I'm not sure how much truth there is in that, but they are both still getting around fine today at the ages of eighty-five and eighty. (Ty Milward)

Rallies and marches against nuclear weapons were an important part of many people's lives in the 1980s. We gathered together, young and old, from all over Britain, to share our fears and hopes about the future and the risk of war. A feature of the marches were the many beautifully made banners, people using traditional skills of collage and needlework to portray our lives and the places we come from – all that is threatened by war. This banner is from Hebden Bridge, Yorkshire, at a CND march in London in October 1985. (Janet Bowstead)

This is a photograph of me on my last trip before retiring, after forty-nine years, about to drive the 12.25 Cardiff–London high-speed train which reached 125 mph. I started on the Great Western Railway during the Second World War cleaning steam engines – that was where all budding drivers had to start. The next step was to become a fireman and after sixteen years of hard, dirty work I became a driver on steam engines. During the 1960s we made the step from steam to diesel. I enjoyed my railway career and once worked the royal train. (Cyril Sedgbeer)

This photo was taken in 1963 – when a group of 'beatniks' from London decided to have a day in the country. The place is a village in Hertfordshire called Bayford, where my Uncle Tony (with banjo) was evacuated as a boy during the Second World War. My Uncle John is next to him playing a guitar. The man in the foreground went on to become a world-famous rock star – his name is Rod Stewart. (Nicholas Truefitt)

Outside the gates of a park in Ashton-Under-Lyne, Lancashire. It was always a treat to buy an ice cream when entering or leaving the park. The two young ladies persuaded the ice cream man to take their photograph on his bike: we like to think of them as the Ladies from Walls selling the Walls delights, the *crème de la crème*. The ice cream van still stands outside the park gates and it's just as nice to have an ice cream on a hot sunny day: some things never change. (Melinda Whalley)

The Bognor Regis World Clown Convention, March 1991. I took this 'happy' shot in front of the town's information office while I was covering the convention for the media. Sadly the clown conventions are no longer held, which is a great pity as the five days brought a lot of laughter into this little Sussex seaside town in the bleak month of March. I'm sure future generations will regret the loss of these fun-filled days. (Richard Cooke)

Tower Colliery opened in 1759; the infamous Crawshay family took over in 1820. After the Merthyr Riots the Crawshays built a tower to protect the family in 1912. The Marquis of Bute took over, and after many strikes and lockouts the pit was nationalised in 1948. In 1969 Tower was one of twelve pits in Wales to support the men's conditions. After years of unrest the whole coalfield went on the 1984–5 great strike. Tower played a leading role. In April 1994 Tower was a profitable pit but was closed by the Government. On 2 January 1995 237 men put their redundancy money together to buy the pit. It is the only pit in the world owned by the workforce. (Dennis Davies)

End of shift. The time was 2.30 p.m. on a winter's day in January 1954, at the end of the day shift. Miners at the Ty-Trist Colliery battle against the elements, crossing the bridge to the lamp room and then dispersing to their respective homes. They were deprived of the luxury of pit-head baths. Instead they had to travel in dirty clothes and with grimy faces. That was their way of life. Five years later the colliery closed for good. That is why this scene is a brief moment in the past which will never be repeated. (Derek Harding, **Runner Up**)

Two draymen delivering beer by barge, 1969. They made this journey once a week pulling a 2 ton load behind them for half a mile along the towpath of the Thames to the Isis Tavern, situated on the banks of the River Thames, near Iffley Lock, Oxford. Why by barge and not lorry? Those who have had the pleasure of a quiet drink at this centuries-old inn will recall the half-mile walk from the nearest road before being able to enjoy it. (Bill Radford)

The harvesting of the hops each year was very much a family event within the village. The smell and stain from the hops stayed with you for days, sometimes weeks. This picture was taken during a break for lunch. Hops are no longer picked by hand; therefore this is a scene from country life in the early twentieth century that has now passed into history. (Roy Gipson)

The poster in the background shows 'Buffbill' (the legendary Buffalo Bill). In the 25 June issue of the *Northern Echo* I found an advertisement for the circus coming to Darlington for one day on 6 July 1904. My great-grandfather, J. Byers, was a master blacksmith in West Auckland, and was also the nephew of George Stephenson, the railway pioneer. (Brian Newby)

This was many years before the National Health Service. A carnival was held in North Ormensy, to raise funds for the provision of a hospital bed and its upkeep, since they depended on charity. This mock wedding in 1926 achieved first prize. My father was dressed as the bride and my mother sat centre right next to the vicar. I was the five-year-old pushed in between them. The people and industry of the district supported the hospitals of that day. Functions like this provided the entertainment as well as raising funds for good causes, as these were hard times. (Kenneth Broomfield, **Overall Winner**)

English Heritage brings history back to life with a series of events and re-enactments at Bolsover Castle, after a £3.6 million renovation, which unveiled magnificent original paintings and fine craftsmanship of that period in the 'little castle', an early seventeenth-century country house built by Sir Charles Cavendish on the site of a medieval castle which dominated the landscape. The person shown here was so engrossed in his part that it was almost as if he believed he was living at that time. (Linda Spivey)

This photograph was taken in 1903 outside a pub near Ongar, Essex. The men in the picture are all related, brothers, uncles and grandfathers. They lived in a row of cottages in Manor Road, Chigwell. It is the wedding day of the man standing behind the two men in the driver's seat. The bridegroom eventually became the father of my wife. (John Cronan)

This picture was taken at Speakers Corner, Hyde Park, in 1980. Speakers Corner is generally recognised as the premier location for free speech. We are accustomed to sunny days, huge crowds and a dutiful police presence, but this picture was taken in the middle of December, immediately following a thunderstorm. It demonstrates that no matter what the weather somebody somewhere will take to his soapbox, and there will always be somebody somewhere who is willing to listen. My picture defines the nature of free speech and captures its essence, the human need to be heard. (John Finnegan, **Winner**)

During the 1990s, after the social and economic upheaval of the 1980s, the *Big Issue* magazine kept the homeless and unemployed from begging. This *Big Issue* seller for several months became as familiar as the street furniture, his preferred pitch being the doorstep of Waterstones booksellers. Sometimes his wife/partner would help out and bring the infant with her. The child would stay for many hours playing with toys scattered about the steps and pavement. Pitches for *Big Issue* sellers are now more closely regulated, and I haven't seen again any child living so conspicuously on the street. (Patrick Anketell-Jones)

A slice of family tradition and social history is captured for future generations to remember. Local farriers Mr Varnam and his son Paul re-shoe a shire horse together. This ancient occupation is still practised and here it is shared by two generations. This skill is mainly connected with the countryside but is photographed here in urban Leicester. (Maria Estevez, **Runner Up**)

This photograph was taken of my grandfather, Joseph Smith, in 1967. He worked as a senior ticket collector at Newcastle Central Station. The photograph, initially taken for a local newspaper article, reflects the pride that my grandfather took in working for British Rail, at a time when British people had confidence and faith in public transport. (Melanie Gardener)

The scene is the seashore at Larne, Co. Antrim, and the figure is my great-grandfather, Houston Clements, encumbered with a yoke. Suspended from the yoke are two buckets filled with white stones from the beach; he was taking them to the 'big house', Drumalis, one of the homes of Sir Hugh and Lady Smiley. Houston Clements and his wife Agnes lived in one of five gate lodges to the estate. The stones are probably for decoration of the garden. Plans are afoot by Larne Council to build flats on the promenade and build a marina. The townspeople are against this. This is why the photograph is of personal and historic interest. (John Saunderson)

My grandparents brought their family from Hereford to London the previous year, an enormous step involving huge changes. Though country children, my father (next to his mother) and Reg (in the cap) had both had rickets – hence the Victorian boots. My grandfather was at Covent Garden by 4.00 a.m. with his horse and cart. Bedtime for him was 7.00 p.m. As a small child I slept on a pillow on an orange box at the end of their bed. We retired together. The shop, destroyed in the war, was rented, Willoughby being a previous owner. No. 177 (now 107) is a small block of flats. (Patricia Lowe)

My grandfather outside his shop. It shows what little grocery shops used to be like. It also shows some of the old adverts – some things still available today. He lived at the back, cooking on a paraffin stove and sitting on orange boxes. My mother took me to visit him weekly, and he would let me choose the tin of fruit we had with evaporated milk for pudding. (Dorothy Ward)

My great-grandmother, Annie Roberts, looks confident yet ladylike here outside her shop in Cleveland Square, Liverpool, c. 1890. She was sent there against her will to help her aunt and uncle as a young girl but eventually took control and improved profits before inheriting the business. She and the square are gone, but in her life she showed that patience and hard work win through in the end. (Wendy Carlson, **Winner**)

Three young fitters fooling around at Ty-Trist Colliery, Tredegar, Gwent. These were the days when they were learning their trade the hard way and for very little money. When the colliery closed in 1959 these boys, along with many others, were forced to seek employment elsewhere. This is one precious moment when their lives came together in hard work and fleeting moments of fun. (Derek Harding)

Oxfordshire Fruit Farm in the 1970s, at the time when the 'pick-your-own-fruit' era was in full swing. On this occasion a young mother had been gently picking her choice of fruit so as not to waken her sleeping baby. The mother in the picture will now be in her fifties and her baby around thirty years of age. (Bill Radford, **Runner Up**)

The photo shows my grandmother (bottom right-hand corner) when she worked voluntarily in the soup kitchen during the Tynewydd colliery 'lock out'. The Rhondda flourished with coal mines at that time, but now only coal tips are left showing their past existence, other than the colliery (non-working) at the Heritage Park, Porth. The photo reflects the hard times endured by the miners and their families, yet shows the true spirit of the community. (Freda Gibbon, **Winner**)

This lady and her brother had a stall in Chapel Market in Islington, London, in 1996. I frequently passed through the market on my rounds as a community nurse. Many of my older patients remembered the original 'Cally' market off Caledonian Road, which one man said was like the poor man's Harrods as you could buy just about anything there. Markets provide a focal point for a community and are often under threat of closure. Perhaps the market tradition will continue to save us all from the characterless and impersonal chain stores. (Catherine Brown)

This photograph took pride of place in our family home in Wimbledon. The thin gentleman in the first row is Mohammed Ali Jinnah, the founder of Pakistan. Sitting next to him in white is our maternal grandfather, and the young man in the tie in the third row is our uncle. It was taken in Jullundar, Northern India, in 1943 when Mr Jinnah visited the Muslim League headquarters. They were working towards independence from the British and indeed from India itself, a goal finally achieved in August 1947. Throughout our childhood our mother talked proudly of her father's involvement in Pakistan's creation and of his friendship with Mr Jinnah. It was not until after our mother's death in 1998 that we realised to our astonishment that the photo extended both left and right to include members of our father's family whom our mother was not keen on. She had, therefore, simply cut them out. (Arfaan Hasan)

My mother (centre) and my two aunties taking their first holiday in peacetime, 1947. Throughout the war years the sisters had often talked of how they would treat themselves to a holiday in Wales when the war ended. Helen, Leah, Lilly, and the remaining two sisters, not shown (Alice and Irene), refer to this photograph as 'happy days'. (Barry Clarke)

A sunny morning in town when traffic was never a problem. Not only was there still petrol rationing, but very few people could afford to buy a car. A brand new shiny car parked in the street tended to attract small boys. They gathered around to admire it in those days, not to scratch the paintwork or try to break in. (Wendy Hobart, **Runner Up**)

A street party in Turnchapel, Plymouth: it was the wedding day of Prince Charles and Lady Diana Spencer. The old traditional street party brings out the old-fashioned games. In this picture you can see the apple dunking game. I am playing, and there is a man waiting to see who's first to pull an apple out of the water with their teeth! I remember the area had many good community values and still had a tuck shop generations old, run from the home of one Peggy Tucker. The area we called the village was shocked by Princess Diana's death. Our memories celebrate her kind spirit. (Carol Lewis)

The title of the photograph is 'Walk On By'. I think it is important, as we pat ourselves on the back that we have reached a new century, that we remember the problems of the homeless and dispossessed still continue. I think future generations will need to be reminded that however sophisticated the society they believe they live in is, human indifference will always be there. (Keith Parmenter Arps)

Deryck and Alison own a farm in Blencogo; the farmhouse is in the picture. In common with other farmers they are experiencing hard times. They had hoped to pass the farm on to son Stuart but now the future is uncertain, and who knows what this new century will bring. The working farmhouse pictured here may become some commuter's country retreat. And future generations may not experience life in a working farming village.
(Geoffrey Prestwich)

My father (on the left) in his first job before joining the army at the age of sixteen, during the First World War. In this photo you get some idea of the style of clothing, the currency and price of food at the time, 1913. Although there was plenty of food in the stores money was scarce, so my grandparents were glad of any bargains my father could get. (Henry Dickson)

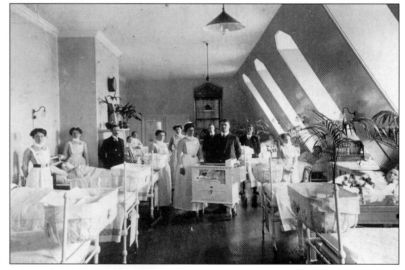

The maternity ward at University College Hospital in 1908. The baby in the incubator is my mother (now ninety-two years old), born prematurely and not expected to survive! The ward, the clothes, the uniforms, the facilities: everything is so changed nowadays. (Dawn Pavitt, **Winner**)

A local baby competition held in 1956, which my eldest brother won. He is the one being held by the woman in the hat (my mum). The event was held at the Highcliffe Castle fête in Dorset. The castle later suffered a fire and became run down but has now been renovated with aid from the national lottery. My mum and dad went on to have three more sons! (Mathew Price)

Taken in 1959 in Wapping, east London, this photograph shows the real horse power that was then still part of everyday life. This brewer's dray was the ideal stop/start transport for local distribution between warehouses and the many public houses in the Dockland area of London. (Philip Belcher)

I like the details of this picture from 1980: the boards advertising nightclubs, 'Thrift' and 'Express Freight'; also the older men in the group, wearing ties and smart jackets. In some ways it's quite hard to date this image. Apart from the hairstyles and the commercial displays, it could easily have been taken twenty or so years earlier. Football grounds look very different now, and this gentle scene is very definitely a thing of the past. Another thing I like is the ambiguity – it's either pre-kick-off, or just another boring game at Feethams. As a long-standing Darlo' fan, I wouldn't bet against the latter. (Michael Pearson)

I don't think you could take a baby to a match now, and the policeman seems superfluous. Unfortunately the general picture for football grounds and terracing changed massively almost two years after this scene, with the football disasters at the Heysel Stadium in Belgium in 1985 and the Bradford City fire. (Michael Pearson)

This picture was taken by my father in 1968. At that time he was a long-distance driver for a well-known haulage firm called Snaylam's of Bolton. When I was a child he used to take me with him on trips the full length of the country. This picture is of me when we were parked up at Tooley Street lorry park, just at the back of Tower Bridge, in the London Borough of Southwark. The lorry park shut down in 1970, and today the area is used mainly for coaches carrying tourists. (Anthony Green)

This photograph, though taken in June 2000, may well have been taken many, many years ago. The ancient town of Whitby in North Yorkshire is well known for its great fishing shanties passed down from fathers to sons over many years. You could well imagine taking a step back in time with the cobbled street and stone pillars of the eighteenth-century Town Hall. The obvious clue to the recent origin of the photograph is the sign offering tapes and CDs for sale. (Harold McEwan)

My grandfather worked on many of the London theatres and was skilled in marbling and graining. He was responsible for many of the beautiful ceilings that can be seen in the old London theatres. Much of this work was carried out using his thumb, which became worn down as a result. Born in 1856, he became a widower in 1907 and raised six children on his own, while continuing to work. As a result of his skill he was awarded the Freedom of the City of London. (Carol Stanley)

My photograph was taken sometime in the late '40s or early '50s in Nottingham. It was quite unposed and the subject was not aware of the camera. Here is a poor old lady presumably earning a few coppers selling newspapers to keep the wolf from the door – better pensions would eliminate this for future generations. Here is resignation, sadness, a reflection on how hard life had been to her. Note how the strip lighting to her hat is balanced by the selection of hats in the window: an example of how the camera can uniquely capture evocative fragments. (Thomas Robert Mayo)

I took part in an anti-hunt demo in 1995: I took quite a lot of photos but this one says it all. About 20,000 people gathered in Hyde Park, then marched to Trafalgar Square where several prominent speakers including Tony Benn voiced their thoughts on hunting. As you can see Trafalgar Square was packed, and a lot of the protesters are young. I like this photo and I think it will interest future generations. Will the marches and protests still be going on in years to come? The ban on hunting seems so near: only time will tell. (F. Gregory)

The closure of the mining industry in the South Wales valleys has been well documented, along with the devastating effects on local communities. To combat some of the effects of poverty and social exclusion, new community initiatives have developed. This photograph shows volunteers delivering recycled furniture to people in need living on one of the housing estates in the valleys. It is a positive image of people choosing unpaid work as an alternative to the negative effects of unemployment. It also demonstrates the growing awareness that recycling can reduce the volume of waste and bring real benefits to the community. (Lynda Davies)

I was able to gain access to the Sikh temple via an Asian friend. Since the 1960s Dudley, West Midlands, has had a very big multicultural population and has a particularly strong Asian group. There are a number of Sikh temples in the area, which to an outsider like me seemed to be a firm part of the structure that enables people to retain their cultural identity while integrating. (Michael Pearson)

One of many photographs taken on holiday by my mother (Mrs B.M. Martin) in Wales. It shows the family having a picnic tea. For lunch they boiled a kettle using sticks, and collected milk from a farm. The photograph shows the dress of the day. The excellent picture was taken using a Kodak camera. My grandmother's hair turned quite white when she was under thirty years old. The car they used was a Citroën. (Richard Martin, **Winner**)

This is a photograph of an ancient Maytime custom in Patterdale (and elsewhere in Britain) and a delightful spectacle at that. I had to record it. (Gwyneth Jones)

This gentleman was enjoying a cup of tea at a Sunday morning car boot sale in Radcliffe, Greater Manchester. His sartorial statement of protest represented a large section of the British population in the early '90s when a tide of frustration and discontent swept out Thatcherism. This proud man with his defiant demeanour and garb is a symbol of north-west Britain under the rule of Margaret Thatcher. (Elizabeth Spencer)

My grandfather William Hamilton (right) standing outside his shop with one of his friends, 1960. The photograph is of personal and historic value as it shows what small businesses were like forty years ago and how they have altered over the years to cater for the ever-changing market. I think that it will interest future generations as it shows how shops have changed dramatically in such a short period of time. (Euan Bennie)

This photo was taken on 24 July 1990, the day the QE2 visited Liverpool. The last liner had sailed out of Liverpool in 1972 and this was the rebirth of the city. It was wondrously hot and everybody, old and young alike, were enjoying themselves. The QE2 has visited four more times but it never lived up to its debut. (Stephen Quinn)

Ironbridge, River Severn, 1960s. Beneath the elegant span of the first iron bridge ever to be built, Mr Eustace Rogers, the local coracle builder, was giving me a demonstration of the manoeuvrability of his boat. The coracle, a primitive portable fishing boat, was first recorded by the Romans. In the 1960s Mr Rogers made his by interlapping laths and covering them with heavy linen. Finally the linen was given several coats of tar. (Cliff Smith)

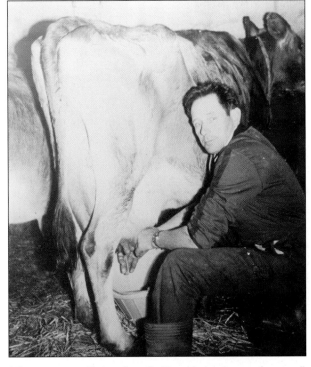

My parents on Margate sea front, 1957. The town's history as a seaside resort dates from the eighteenth century and lays claim to being the first British resort to popularise donkey rides, in the early nineteenth century. As this picture illustrates, my parents are preserving memories of a fun day out courtesy of a snapshot photographer and his props. The increasing accessibility of travel abroad in the following decades saw a waning in popularity of the British seaside resort, but this photo captures it in its heyday. (Lorraine Morley, **Winner**)

This is my grandfather, Roy Cudlipp. He has been a farmer all his life, and my father also took on the farm when he left school. I believe this photo shows how farming has always been a huge part of Jersey life, although sadly there are not many farmers left. It symbolises part of British history and how the world is changing. My grandfather is now older and still works on the farm, because he says if he didn't he would miss it and would be bored, as it has always been his life. (Ella Cudlipp)

Quarry Hill flats were built in Leeds during the 1930s to house over 3,000 working-class people. Famous for its modernist looks, lifts and waste disposal system, it was near to factories and shops and the city. By the 1960s it had become a problem for the City Fathers and the new-look Leeds. It was demolished, and the main computer centre for the National Health Service and DHSS now occupies half the site. The remainder is still up for sale! The photograph depicts the last arch of Quarry Hill Flats with the men who took it all away. A short time later a lot of Leeds housing went into negative equity. (Peter Mitchell)

These protesters were lying down in the roadway to stop contractors' vehicles commencing work on the M11 relief motorway as fast as police were forcibly removing them. In the background all the dog wanted to do was play. (Anthony Kaye)

An icebreaker on the Wolverhampton–Birmingham Canal, 1963. The icebreaker's timbers were protected by strong metal sheathing and the shape of the hull enables the boat to be rocked by the gang who man her. Rocking cracks the ice: if the boat was just pulled it would only break a channel its own width or leave the water and slide out on top of the ice. After the 1963 freeze-up small icebreakers were in use, towed by tractors where the towpath permitted. Unfortunately freezing conditions persisted and few boats were used commercially after the thaw. (Cliff Smith)

Albert Braund was born in the Devon fishing hamlet of Bucks Mills in 1863. He was one of seven generations of fishermen, stretching from his great-grandfather Joseph to his great-grandson, who is still fishing today. Here Albert is passing on the traditional craft of making withy lobster pots to his son, Bert. The personal significance of this photograph is that it depicts members of my family carrying out their trade, a trade which I follow. Its wider historical interest comes from the portrayal of a dying way of life, which saw sons following the calling of their forefathers. (Christopher Braund)

These Romany Gipsy families were the last to live in horse-drawn caravans in the south of England. They are seen here in 1964 before being housed by the local authority. (Tony Boxall)

Seahenge was discovered by a local resident in September 1998. In June 1999 English Heritage decided to excavate and remove the wooden circle. This was done with little consultation. Locals including myself had been aware of this monument in our ancient Norfolk landscape for generations. To the druids it represented a sacred and ritually significant moment of our ancestors. The emotions that this issue raised clearly demonstrated that our history is not perceived as belonging to the people but to those in authority. It is therefore imperative that future generations debate and judge this act. (Jason Dawson, **Runner Up**)

Our local street party to celebrate the wedding of Prince Charles and Lady Diana. It was a lovely hot sunny day and a very joyous occasion. The celebration went on until late with music and dancing. What a shame the occasion had such a disastrous outcome. (Ann O'Neil)

Right: This young man was my father-in-law, William Bruce, known as Bob. Born in Attercliffe, Sheffield, on 8 November 1909, he died on 28 March 2000. Bob lived through two world wars. He married his wife Hilda in 1932 and they were married for sixty-seven years; they had thirteen children, all of whom are still living. He worked long hours as a boiler man at the waterworks to support his large family, to whom he was devoted, and on his death this year he left fifty-four descendants. Bob was truly a twentieth-century man, who lived for more than nine-tenths of it. (Margaret Bruce)

Picnics featured quite often during my childhood, although I wasn't present on this occasion. Most summer weekends would involve the whole family travelling to somewhere in the county of Norfolk. This picture was taken by my Uncle Derrick at a favourite location, Weybourne, near to the sea in north Norfolk. The picnics were packed into an old leather suitcase. We never ate sandwiches: all the ingredients, salads, meats, etc., would be served on plates. Afterwards grandfather would boil water on the primus stove. We then had hot tea with grandmother's homemade shortcakes, which to my delight would be heavily impregnated with raisins or sultanas. (Nigel Gooch)

I was brought up in this street: I'm dancing with childhood friends. I'm in the centre next to the girl wearing a gingham dress, back row. The party was celebrating King George VI's coronation. Times were very hard, living in two upstairs rooms with five in the family – no water upstairs and an outside toilet. I was lucky, going on a summer holiday with the Children's Country Holiday Fund when I was ten years old. (Clarissa Bourne)

Traditional retailing on the verge of extinction. This is Holt's boot store, purveyor of the legendary Dr Marten boot, Tottenham Court Road, London. There are no computers, no mood music, no youthful sales staff, just old blokes with racks of boots in cardboard boxes. Despite the perennial trendiness of Dr Marten's boots, it's hard to say how long shops like this can survive in the face of the homogenisation of the high street. (John Carroll)

In 1890 a photograph was taken of my great-great-grandfather (standing third from the right) on a farm in the countryside. He worked on the farm when the industrial revolution was at its peak. In the background is an old machine, used for separating seeds from the stalks of corn. My photograph has personal value because it shows me what one of my ancestors looked like and what job he did. Future generations will learn how people used to do all the work on farms until machinery took over. (Laura Freeman, Winnersh Primary School)

Eco warriors protest against the destruction of woodland for road and housing development. They build their homes in trees and tunnel underground in an attempt to obstruct the destruction. At Rettendon they stayed underground for forty days. The previous record of twenty-two days was held by Disco Dave at Manchester Airport. It is my belief that they will be seen in years to come as great environmentalists. Many local residents and police officers become fond of them even though their demonstrations are often unlawful. (Nicky Lewin)

On Friday 13 June 1941 I was radio officer aboard the SS *Tresillion*. We were torpedoed and sunk by a U-boat. After five days in the North Atlantic we were rescued by the American SS *Duane*. America was still neutral at that time, so took us to Canada. My wife had the hell of a 'listed lost' letter but we were eventually reunited. This close-up of our rescue may interest other survivors or their families. I am the one holding the oar pointing to sea. Aged eighty-nine, I still thank God for that American crew who saved my life. (Richard Davison)

Sandor Lengyel at Markeaton Park in 1959. He arrived in Britain in January 1957, a refugee from the 1956 Hungarian Revolution. We met the same year: I was seventeen years old and I would not go out with him as his English was not much good and we could not converse. As you can see two years on he was reading the *Daily Express*. We met again three years later and married in 1961. He was a Telecom technician. To this day we still have a *Daily* and *Sunday Express*. (P.K. Lengyel, **Winner**)

Roddie Clark, born in a 'barrow top' vardo (caravan) in Donkey Row, Carr Street, East End, 1919. The name Donkey Row originated because a costermonger lived in almost every house on the street. Roddie described his life as a Cockney Romany costermonger as 'every Sunday morning since I was a young "chevy" [child] I come down to Brick Lane except during the war, to sell my "tom foolery" [jewellery], to earn myself a "cushty luvver" [good money] and to "chew the fat" [have a chat]'. This image is already a historical event. (Jo McGuire)

Alfred Frederick Green was born in Lincoln on 9 July 1912. When leaving Sincil Bank School at fourteen he was given the advice 'people will always need bread', so became an apprentice baker at Chatterton's in Lincoln. Like all apprentices in those days he started by making local deliveries on the firm's bike. Alf went on to become a master baker. On 9 April 1984 Alf went as usual to the Liberal Club – a few pounds in the one arm bandit, maybe a game of bingo, certainly a few pints of mild. On the way home Alf collapsed and although a young constable administered mouth to mouth when the ambulance got him to Lincoln County Hospital he was pronounced dead on arrival. (Arthur Bilton)

There is no birth date, no fixed address, yet no fair or market would be complete without the presence of the 'Gypsy King' Kevin Price. Almost every Sunday morning Kevin's flamboyant attire, cowboy hat and vivid handkerchief add vitality to the markets in Brick Lane, east London. This image is of historical value, for in the true Romany way of life few lines are written; the face is the untold story. (Jo McGuire)

Me and my future wife Pat Barling on my 500cc Matchless. The photo was taken on the way to Worthing during the summer of 1951. She is eighteen and I am twenty-one. In company with about a dozen other bikers we set off to the coast every Sunday morning, rain or shine. Every Thursday night we went to Wembley Speedway. Our heroes were Bill Kitchen, Tommy Price, Split Waterman and Broncho Wilson. The stadium was packed with fans eager to see the home riders win. It was great fun, and this photograph sums up those magical sap-rising days of youth for an old buffer who now drives a Volvo. (Gordon K. Marriott)

This traditional family photograph was taken to commemorate my fifty-seventh birthday and shows my six grandchildren Charlotte, James, Harriet, William, Matthew and Megan, who are to join in the celebrations. What it cannot show is the ongoing changes and opportunities in many modern women's lives which enabled me to return to education at a mature age and this year to realise my ambition of obtaining a master's degree in local history. No sitting in a corner in a rocking chair yet awhile! (Carol Powell)

My grandmother Fanny and great-aunt Eliza are picnicking in a Surrey house not far from Dorking in 1902. My grandparents, poor south Londoners, owned what they called a 'larn dry'. Grandma washed the clothes and Grandpa (Henry Moorhouse Lymbery) delivered the clean laundry on his horse and cart. Picnics, rare treats, were only possible because of the horse and cart. The outings were an example of a break for many whose lives were lived in unbroken drudgery. The picture was taken by my father, who went on to become a pioneering Fleet Street photographer. (E. Lymbery)

My mother, father, sister and I are watching Lloyd George and Megan Lloyd George leaving the unemployed centre in Jarrow. Father was among the many unemployed men who lost their jobs when Palmers shipyard was closed. Crowds gathered at the street corners to give Mr Lloyd George a truly amazing welcome. The man and woman holding the children are my mother and father and the children are me and my twin sister Margaret. The photograph holds significance for me as it is so far away from the unkempt bare-footed image that many have of the unemployed in the years of the depression. (Winifred Gray)

At the end of Worthing Pier in the summer of 1977, the year of the Queen's Silver Jubilee. Worthing Pier was originally built in 1862 and subsequently enlarged in 1889. The pier was severely damaged in the great storm in 1913, but it was rebuilt and reopened in 1914. The building featured in the photo is now a nightclub. The piers remaining at our coastal towns and resorts are now very precious relics of our past, and we must maintain and preserve them. (Tony Jones)

I was a postgraduate student at Leeds University and my wife (we were both twenty-one) was in her first teaching job at Quarry Mount School – the building at the top of the hill in the picture. We had both been born and raised in a leafy and prosperous area of Bournemouth so these cobbled streets of gardenless back to backs, with washing strung across the road, were fascinatingly different. The younger kids in the picture were at my wife Sylvia's school. There was no vandalism! I am struck by the cleanness of the street. (John Dinham, **Winner**)

The Shrovetide football match dates back to the reign of King Henry II. It typifies an eccentric side of British culture and has an atmosphere of pride and heritage. One can imagine the ghosts of past players jumping and screaming at relatives to strive harder than is physically possible. It seems that such spirits are driving the two centre characters. They could be placed in another period without so much as a blink. This is an example of how tradition is unaffected by time. (Chris Dyer)

My grandma Rose standing outside the nursing home where she lived for three years while training to be a nurse. She really enjoyed her job and was top of her class in nursing school. This photo is important to me because she died of cancer when I was only eighteen months old, so I don't remember her. This photo was taken in 1956 and shows what nurses' uniforms looked like then, so we can see how much they've changed over time. (Rebecca Louise Ryan, Ysgol Pencoed, **Secondary School Winner**)

Real ironmongers' shops predate plastic packaging. A single nail would be wrapped in a twist of paper. Pink paraffin was stored in a tank to the right of the picture; customers filled their paraffin bottles from its tap. Paraffin heaters warmed the draughts that a coal fire couldn't reach. Soon after this photo was taken plastic buckets replaced galvanised pails and ironmongers' shops became hardware stores. The shop had been purchased by my grandfather in the 1870s. The previous owners had gone to the gold rush – they may have been a bit late! (Barbara Hyslop)

This photograph reminds me of what I was like at that age – running wild in the street getting into all sorts of mischief. The car had been dumped by some joyrider; some bored kid must have set it on fire for kicks. When the firefighters got there and put out the fire, the fireman sprayed some of the kids taking in the scene as a joke. It was a hot day, but he got more than he bargained for as the youths tried to exact some revenge. In the future will children be let out of the home, to get up to this kind of thing? (Alan Ainsworth, **Runner Up**)

This photograph, taken in Blackpool in 1945, is of a group of girls all employed by Vernons Pools, Liverpool. (I am on the front row in the dark dress.) We are all 'Miss Efficiency Girls' – that is, girls who were selected (because of good work, good timekeeping and good attendance) to go for a week's holiday to Blackpool, all expenses paid and staying in a hotel owned by Vernons. We really did enjoy ourselves – lovely hotel, good meals, a visit to the theatre, Blackpool Tower, a day out to the Lakes, and free tickets for all the attractions at the funfair. Happy carefree days! (Georgina Stewart)

inventions

My brother, Jim Colburn, demonstrating something completely new. The year was 1947 and the idea of having a telephone in your car was difficult to believe. My father, a garage and taxi proprietor, thought it might save petrol (a couple of bob a gallon!). Anyway, he ordered it. We were the fourth firm in Britain to have it installed by a well-known Cambridge telecommunications company. I remember, even in 1950, looking in the rear mirror and watching a fare peering back through the window searching for wires as I received radio messages on the phone. (Arthur Colburn, **Winner**)

An old-fashioned fire engine. It is special to me because my dad used to be in the fire service. The photograph was taken in Duxford. The engine is a Leyland Cub FK8 pump. Its colours are maroon and red, which are now the Leicester and Rutland Fire Service colours. It was supplied new to Loughborough in 1939. Its wheeled escape has now been replaced by hydraulic platforms. (David Edwards, Applegrove Primary School)

Here is a typical holiday caravan from the first half of the twentieth century. In appearance it resembles a gypsy caravan and has the added advantage of a canvas awning. It is interesting to compare this with the wide variety of modern, attractive and luxurious holiday homes-on-wheels that families now use in pursuit of a leisure-time activity that has existed for almost as long as the wheel, and will probably continue to appeal throughout the next century and beyond. (Thomas Taylor, Ashville College)

Great-grandad Thomas Douglas Hawkes in the 1920s. He is showing off his new car, a Belsize. These are no longer made today. It had no roof (so he is warmly dressed), an unusual horn, a small door and big wheels. This is an important photo as the car was the first in our family. The photo records technological change as cars are much improved today. This car was probably one of the first to be mass produced. (Laura Miller, Craigholme School, **Secondary School Winner**)

I chose a picture of Bristol Balloon Fiesta, because it shows how popular balloons are today. Even though hot air balloons were made hundreds of years ago, they are still one of the great wonders of the skies. This picture is of the Bristol Balloon Fiesta about eight years ago. Since then even I have been in a balloon! Every year now hundreds of hot air balloons go up into the sky, but when the Fiesta first began it only had a handful of balloons. I think this is a classic picture. (Jessica Atherton, Clifton High School)

This photo is very important to me because I invented this go-kart made from wood and plastic which I rescued. It is environmentally very friendly. It has working lights and indicators, controlled from inside. When I can work out how to fit a clutch, I want to install a lawnmower engine. When I am older I want to be an inventor. Scotland has a good reputation for inventing things – Alexander Graham Bell, John Dunlop and Logie Baird were world beaters. My aim is to invent a generator which does not use fuel. I will one day! (Joe White, Duncanrig Secondary School, **Secondary School Winner**)

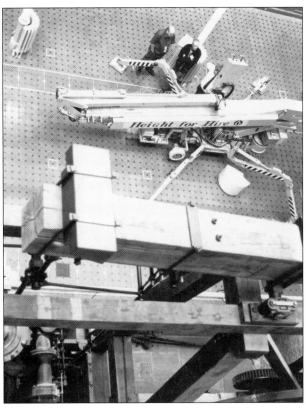

This photograph was taken at the Edinburgh Royal Museum and shows an improbable encounter between past and present engineering. Here is the latest state of the art lifting machine working right next to a steam engine dating from the late eighteenth century. In a few decades from now the complex mechanism of the electric crane might end in a museum too – who knows? (Le Gall Martial)

A Halesom motorcycle, rebuilt and in perfect running order. I was told there are only three of this type of bike left in the country. This motorcycle is a piece of British motor history. The gentleman here has spent a lot of time and money preserving this motorcycle for the future. (Peter John Harper)

The float in this photograph won a Teignmouth Carnival in the 1930s. Its historical importance is that it commemorates Amy Johnson's first Britain–Australia flight; she was the first woman to make this trip. Amy died in 1941 when flying for the Air Transport Auxiliary Service over the Thames. It is of importance to my family because it is my grandmother, dressed as Amy, accompanied by my great-uncle, dressed as a mechanic. It will retain its importance for future generations because Amy was a major historical figure of the twentieth century. For my family this photograph will always represent a cherished moment in our history. (David Richard Graham Birch, Hazeldown Primary School)

In an age of colour television, satellite and cable we sometimes forget that once we only had black and white, three channels and no video recorder. My father loved 9.5 ciné films – Laurel and Hardy, Charlie Chaplin, and so on – and in the winter months it was a useful addition to the TV. In the photograph I believe he is carrying out maintenance: the bulb would get very hot and attract dust so it had to be cleaned, as did the heads and film feeds. (Colin Jagger, **Runner Up**)

This is from a scrapbook of photos taken by my father, who served in the RAF in 1923. The caption on the back is 'Flt Lt Blake attempting to fly round the world landed at 216 Squadron Heliopolis'. I think it is of historic value to future generations to remember the days when attempting to fly round the world was an arduous task. (Pauline Morris, **Runner Up**)

Thomas Scott, my grandfather, repairing his bicycle in the early 1940s. It was safe on the road at that time as cars were few and far between. In fact, when I went out with my parents on our bikes, my mother got off her bike and walked whenever a car appeared in the distance. (David Newsome)

This is my friend Tom Lawton. He's holding his invention 'Wakeyoo', the alarm clock which will revolutionise the way we wake up. Press the button on your 'Wakeyoo' and it will digitally record twenty seconds of sound to your choosing.
Tom wants to wake up to the sound of cows mooing. Here he is pictured recording them in his local farmyard. 'Wakeyoo' is being marketed nationally, is currently being manufactured in Hong Kong, and should be in the shops in October 2000. Historically speaking Tom's invention is going to take the 'alarm' out of alarm clock, and has been entirely developed in virtual reality.
(Paul O'Connor)

I remember my pedal-powered railway engine was an object of great admiration from other boys, who all wanted a ride. You can see the whistle which the driver could blow (on a chain it pulled out of the steam dome). Being an engine driver was about the most exciting thing you could think of. Going to the local park meant crossing two roads – safe then. In the background left, asparagus fern was allowed to grow – I don't suppose working-class families actually ate it! (Philip Fowler)

This is the world land speed record holder: 763.035 mph. I was lucky enough to watch the building of this fantastic vehicle at G-force, Fontwell, West Sussex, even having the chance to sit in the cockpit prior to fabrication. I took this photo at the Goodwood Festival of Speed 2000, only a few miles from where Thrust SSC was built. I am sure future generations will look with awe when they see photographs such as this and remember that this was the first car to break the sound barrier on land. (Richard Cooke)

This year (2000) sees the thirtieth birthday of the Land Rover group and also sees the twenty-fifth anniversary of Range Rovers in police service. In 1975 the Central Police Motorway Group placed the first ever-fleet order, but Lincolnshire Police were the first to receive a delivery of two cars. The vehicle depicted is the Range Rover of today, not a traffic car but an armed-response vehicle from Greater Manchester Police. (Julian Berry)

My grandad had a bike like this when he was younger, and I couldn't resist taking a photo to show my friends. It's amazing how different they are now! (Helen Thake, **Runner Up**)

The Irish Sea blows its winter storms on to Blackpool beach. The sea and salt blow on to the timeless tramway that keeps on going, with its ageless dinosaurs that require little major mechanical maintenance. Trams are always different: no two look the same. Although the seasons change, the trams never stop running. (Des Omurcho)

The prototype Spitfire flew from Eastleigh Airport, Southampton, on 5 March 1936. This photograph shows fourteen of the world's remaining Spitfires flying over Southampton on 4 June 2000, in a magnificent celebration of our aviation heritage. This flight captured the spirit and magic of the glory days and the bravery and dedication of the Battle of Britain pilots. This mass formation commemorates the sixtieth anniversary of the Battle of Britain. I took this photograph as the planes were silhouetted against the blue summer sky, and as I did so I whispered a silent 'thank you' to our past heroes. (Richard Cooke)

It's 1911 and the heavy industry of the Black Country is in full swing. They are making the iron anchor chain for the most technically advanced ship of her day, *Titanic*, not knowing that, just like the ship, the Black Country's heavy industry will not last forever. There is one link on show in the Black Country Living Museum. (Gary Bourne)

A traction engine in full working order. The gent on the right told me he has been rebuilding it over a ten-year period. Most of these engines have now been sold abroad. These two men have spent their lifetime working with and rebuilding these marvels of yesteryear. (Peter John Harper, **Runner Up**)

Returning to its spiritual home, the trimaran *Adventurer* moors on the quayside at Newcastle upon Tyne. It holds the record for the fastest circumnavigation of the world – seventy-four days, twenty hours, fifty-eight minutes. The main hull design is based on the *Turbinia*, designed by the Tyneside engineer Sir Charles Parsons in 1894. The *Turbinia* was the world's first steam turbine-driven ship and also the fastest until 1899. The *Adventurer*'s engines were 350 bhp built by Cummins at nearby Darlington. (Raymond Urwin)

A picture of me, aged 15¾, impatiently waiting to sit my motorcycle driving test at sixteen. I bought the bike through the local paper for £7 10s 0d, a lot of money then. It was very low in power so I took it to bits to find the piston was the wrong way round in the cylinder. The machine was a 1932 two-stroke Coventry-Eagle. On re-assembly it was a real flyer: top speed 38 mph! The observant will notice the outside flywheel, just forward of my shoe. You had to keep your foot away, as it tended to wear out your shoes. (Brian Barnett)

A unique family photo celebrating the early days of civilian flights. It was taken in July 1924 by my mother. The Fokker Friendship had just landed at Heston – consisting of a grass runway, a couple of hangars, a small control tower and a wooden shed for customs, immigration and cargo. From these humble beginnings the airfield would eventually evolve into the mighty complex Heathrow is today. My mother posted the photo to a friend in Berlin and wrote that they would not be staying long in London, as it was 'black, dirty and had a smoggy atmosphere'. (Robert Broeder, **Winner**)

My late husband, Alick Cole, worked as a technician at the Cable & Wireless headquarters on the embankment in London. Here he is sending one of the first commercial wireless pictures to the USA, 1935. Transmission of news pictures by radio was a major technical innovation; three days by transatlantic liner was the alternative. The equipment was massive and the scanning was slow. These developments led to the fast computer scanning which we use now to send pictures around the world by internet and satellite links. (Dorothy Cole, **Winner**)

The photograph is of personal and historic value as it portrays a mode of transport and style of dress (my father's plus-four trousers) no longer seen. With other Clarion Cycling Club members my parents would tour the countryside and in particular the Lake District to escape the humdrum life of the weaving mills and mill-towns. These excursions included camping and cycling trips as far as Ireland, all done by people power. I am sure the picture will be of interest to future generations if only for the curiosity value of the cycle. (Thomas Hill, **Runner Up**)

John Roberts was a very experienced motor engineer. In 1954 he purchased a scrapped 1925 Armstrong Siddeley for £40 and commenced to restore it. Eventually, after having much time, patience and love lavished upon it, it emerged in all its former glory. This car still runs today and his son, Anthony (who is a member of the Great Britain Classic Car Club), attends rallies with it. People such as Mr Roberts deserve to be afforded recognition for their interest, talent and patience. (Barry Williams)

A friend who came to visit and show off his two-seater microcar, a Messerschmitt Tiger, which was very popular in the late '50s and early '60s – being slightly more practical than the Vespas, Lambrettas and other scooters of those days. It was an economical first car and although causing a certain amount of merriment (large owners seemed to wrap it round them rather than get in) proved a success. Something along these lines is surely due for a comeback. (Wendy Hobart)

A tin bath and washboard were in the house when I was young, but not used. We had a modern electric washing machine with a mangle. This was soon replaced by the invention of the spindryer. Our second-hand spinner, however, needed some adjustment. To prevent this roaring machine from dancing around the room and sending water everywhere my mother had to kneel on top and hold tight. (Maureen Perkins)

This photograph captures the beginning of public transport when travel on a charabanc was an adventure. My great-great-uncle looked quite calm, but I'm sure he felt quite apprehensive riding in something that sped along at unheard-of speeds. (Jean Griffiths)

'A bit of welly'. This must be the ultimate in recycling and conservation. The rubber soles of a wellington boot caused the gate to be self closing. On the gate itself, nothing was wasted. (Ken Waugh, **Runner Up**)

Left: Not quite the London Eye, but this big wheel was frighteningly high to a young girl in the 1950s at the Hoppings in Newcastle's Town Moor. This fair originated in a temperance festival dating from 1882, held as a sober alternative to Race Week. Schools were given a holiday and people from miles around flocked to 'the town'. The Hoppings are still very popular, especially the frightening rides. Human nature does not change, but technology provides ever more sophisticated ways to enjoy our fear. (Dorothy Rand, **Runner Up**)

My father, Les Emmans, ran a local dance band prior to the Second World War. When the band broke up, as its members left to join the forces, he built an amplifier, equipped it with speakers, a microphone and a 78 rpm turntable, and became what must have been one of the very first disc jockeys. He introduced and played 78s for dancing at garden parties and local dance halls in Norfolk until he was himself called up. During his service in the RAF he was mentioned in dispatches twice for his innovative work in designing and making training equipment for bomber pilots. (Edward Emmans)

The bicycle was an ideal way for townspeople to visit the countryside in the late 1940s. The countryside was within easy reach of the Black Country. My great-aunt (third from the left) worked in the Philips cycle factory, Smethwick, manufacturing the bikes shown in the photo. For the exhibition at Earls Court, she made a bike that did not have conventional brakes; you stopped by pedalling backwards. The photo shows the friend's farm we used to visit. The ham we are bringing back was home-cured from the pigs on the farm, and was very welcome just after the war. (Kenneth Reynolds)

My father's dispensary, in his chemist's shop, late 1940s. Ingredients were all in powder or liquid form and were kept in individual bottles, and then made up for prescriptions. The small cupboard was lockable and used for storing dangerous drugs. He also made and sold his own cough mixture and hand cream, both of which were very popular in the town. Modern drugs are of course all pre-packaged. The shop was part of our lives: we lived above it and frequently watched him make up prescriptions and help customers with their toiletry purchases. (Catherine Parsons)

An alternative view of the Humber Bridge, taken from the north bank of the river. A remarkable feat of twentieth-century engineering, it was the longest single span suspension bridge in the world when it opened in 1981. Built to encourage financial investment in Humberside, it replaced the beloved paddle steamers which had ploughed the Humber for many years. Born and bred in the city of Hull, I, like many others, mourned the passing of the Humber ferry. For me, the Humber Bridge now signifies that I am almost home whenever I return for a visit. (Pamela Belby)

My father Eric Clench aged fourteen, standing near one of Morris's first lorries with solid tyres, 1926. The lorry was owned by Nathaniel Henry Irving, a close relative of Henry Irving the poet whose statue is in the Main Street, Dumfries. N.H. Irving married my grandfather's sister. The lorry was used in his business, which supplied the butchery trade with all the requisites they needed, such as paper bags, greaseproof paper, string, hooks, skewers, knives and even sausage skins. (Margaret Howard)

Members of the 1970s Morris Motors car factory fire brigade at Cowley, Oxford, wore false moustaches and donned original old uniforms and helmets to show off their lovely 1920s fire-engine. It was taken from the works museum (which does not now exist) for this historical photo of 1970. Note the long handbrake lever and wooden brake shoed on the wooden spoked wheels of this horse-drawn fire engine. Sadly the factory was closed and razed to the ground in the early part of 1990, leaving thousands of car workers unemployed. (Bill Radford)

My late father, William Bennett of Bow, east London, in the foreground, carrying out some of the repair work to Big Ben, the clocktower of the Houses of Parliament. It was carried out after a survey to see what had to be done to repair war damage. At the same time the opportunity was taken to overhaul the clock mechanism. The ornamentation work and the finial were also re-gilded by hand using gold leaf, a practice last carried out on the tower in 1881. (Stephen Bennett, **Sky Digital Winner**)

The picture shows my mum at the age of nineteen rolling rock in a rock factory. Now rock is rarely made by hand. Factories usually have machines to make products. The picture also shows us the type of jobs people of this age had, and the clothes they wore for them. (James McAlonan, Lytham St Anne's High School, **Secondary School Winner**)

The Avro Vulcan delta wing bomber was developed in the late 1940s. The first flight took place on 30 August 1952 and the RAF took delivery of the first squadron in May 1957. One hundred and twenty were built through to 1964. None took part in active duty until they were brought out of retirement in April 1982, when they took part in the bombing of Port Stanley Airfield in the Falklands War. The sixteen-hour missions involved 8,000-mile round trips from Ascension Island – the longest in the history of warfare. This is thought to be the last flying example. (Ronald Sumner)

The SUPREME SUNBEAM

1.000 H.P. CAR,
BUILT BY
THE SUNBEAM MOTOR CAR C° L°
WOLVERHAMPTON
ENGLAND

207 M.P.H.
Timed over a 5 Kilometre course
March 29th 1927

My great-grandad was foreman on the building of the 1000 hp Sunbeam which was the first car to exceed 200 mph, at Daytona Beach, USA, in 1927. It was driven by Major Henry Segrave. My great-grandad also worked on the 2-litre Sunbeam that won the French Grand Prix in 1923. On more than one occasion he went down to Portsmouth and the Isle of Wight to test yacht engines for the royal family. The photograph is of significance because the car forms part of the history of the world land speed record. (Thomas Bunce, The Kingswinford School)

This photograph, given to me by the works foreman in 1950, provides an intriguing glimpse of a small gasworks in a Devon town, Tavistock, at the turn of the twentieth century. A new gasworks opened on a larger site in 1906, where gas working ceased in 1956. In the photo Absalom Francis, engineer, works at the original site in Gas House Lane. Note the water wheel, which provided the power to transfer gas from the retorts, through the purification stage and into the gasholders. In the new works this essential plant was steam powered. (Michael Parriss)

This photograph was taken in the Virgin record shop in Belfast. I was going to the first floor and was struck by the expressions of the three young men – all totally engrossed in their own worlds, oblivious to anything around them including the photographer. While we have seen enormous technological advancement in the year 2000, one cannot help thinking we have lost something special in face to face communication. This picture forces us to question the advance of technology and the impact it will have on future generations. I developed the photograph myself in the very cramped conditions of a broom cupboard! (Phyllis McFarlane)

The invention of the car has brought many social changes. The photo shows one of our first Ford cars on our way to Devon, on holiday, as the suitcase in the boot shows. Journeys took many hours, as no motorways had been built. Cars were still mostly black – as Henry Ford said when he introduced mass production, 'any colour as long as it's black'. The roads were much quieter as many people still relied on charabanc or train. Even the AA patrol men, with their motorbike and sidecar, had time to salute when they saw a member's badge on the car. (Kenneth Reynolds)

My four children, Tom, Louis, Joe and Elsa, in March 2000. They adored the computer when it arrived at Christmas 1999. They were glued to it for some time. Now thankfully it has just occasional rather than constant use. I feel it is important in the future for parents and teachers to regulate the time a child sits in front of computers and televisions, allowing them time to discover their natural environment and the outside world, rather than being tied to a screen for stimulation and information. (Joanna Rice)

Are you certain there was an engine in here this morning? I caught three members of the Beamish museum staff trying to mend this veteran car, which had broken down on its first morning run. We were on a day trip to the museum, which we all enjoyed. Beamish certainly gives a good impression of life in the past. (Ronald Pears)

This photograph was taken in 1922, the occasion being a charabanc trip from Macclesfield to Matlock. My grandmother aged fourteen is pictured sitting fourth from the front. In those days a bumpy four-hour drive in your Sunday best, with the wind in your hair and the sound of the engine purring loudly, was all part of the excitement of actually getting there. Of course it would take an hour today. Somehow I think she had a more thrilling and more memorable day trip to Derbyshire than I had last time I travelled there by car! (Darren Rowbotham)

Technology comes to the fire brigade – the first motorised engine in Yeovil. Men dedicated to saving life, unpaid, put their courage and skills and very little else up against the terror of fire to help others and to save lives. Grandad Dover (front passenger seat), grandad Warry (on the tender at the back), both volunteers to the brigade, show off their new equipment. (Roderick Dover)

In the age of digital television, modern telephone communications and the internet, this photograph is a symbol of modern technology. It shows the first satellite dish built at Goonhilly Earth Station in Cornwall. Named Arthur, it received the first signals sent from the Telstar satellite launched in 1962. It is still used occasionally. The Earth Station now has many dishes that receive communications from all over the world. For example, a news report transmitted from the Middle East can travel via a satellite to Goonhilly and reach your television set in seconds. (Marilynne Tom)

The car in the foreground is my dad's Gilbern. This is important to me because it was the first car ever produced in Wales. The logo for the car is none other than the Welsh dragon. It was produced by two men called Giles Smith and Bernard Frieze. The name Gilbern is made up of the start of both their names, Gil for Giles and Bern for Bernard. It is also important to me because it's pure Welsh, and because there are only about a hundred left. So that is why I think this is very important to my history and many others as well. (Rhys Morgan, Ysgol Pencoed)

This photograph is of my dad and his friend Peter when they were builders together about twenty years ago. They are making a hole to put a 7 foot doorway into a big building in York. My dad is holding the jackhammer. My dad told me that it was very heavy and it made a loud noise. It is powered by electricity and you can see the wire going downwards. I like the photo because I like machinery. It will be interesting in the future because builders might not have this hammer to knock walls down. (Joshua Hughes, St Wilfrid's RC Primary)

My grandfather, Joseph Nwaneri Iheme. He was born in 1930 and died in 1995. The photo shows him doing some building work. I think it is of historical significance as if you look closely at the bottom left-hand side of the picture you get an idea of how high up he is. He wore no harness and there was nothing to break his fall. This, I think, just shows the great advances in technology, which allow safer work to be done and make it easier at the same time. The photo was taken in Nigeria between 1962 and 1964. (Obinna Henry Nnajiuba, Coopers Company & Coborn School, **Secondary School Winner**)

war & peace

When the American aircraft carrier USS *Philippine Sea* visited Malta in 1948 the occasion was marked by a Port Rifle Meeting, US Marines vs British Army, Royal Navy and Royal Marines. The photo shows me, then Leading Wren Carden (representing the navy teams), four US Marines, a British Army sergeant and a Royal Marine sergeant (42 Commando). In 1948 women were not exactly second class citizens but definitely inferior to men. So apart from my own team two hundred-odd men knew I could not possibly shoot well. I enjoyed standing up for women and proving the men were wrong. (Heather Edwards)

My grandfather Trefor Jones, aged twenty-four. After the declaration of the Second World War he joined the RAF and was posted in Egypt for four and a half years. After the war he returned home to rejoin his wife. Many war stories were told to my mother and her brothers, including the capture of an Italian prisoner, Angelo, who became not only the cook for the British soldiers but also a friend. Although I never met my grandfather, I have heard stories of how brave and courageous he was during the war in fighting for his country. (Rhian Nerys Locke, Aberdare Girls' School, **Secondary School Winner**)

The man on the left is my grandfather, seen here in 1939, just before the start of the Second World War. He was on sentry duty after exercises. He was eighteen years of age when he went into the Royal West Kent Army Barracks. You can see in this picture what kind of clothes soldiers had to wear during the war. They must have been quite heavy to run around in all day. The gun must have been quite heavy as well. (Tessa Qizilbash, Ashford School, **Secondary School Winner**)

My father took this picture in May 1940. We were on holiday in Bournemouth and had made friends with some French soldiers recently evacuated from Dunkirk. It marks a turning point in the history of both Britain and the Field family, as very soon the harsh realities of war changed peaceful scenes like this with barbed wire, sandbags and the ugly clutter of war. At home in Manchester the family endured the Blitz of December 1940, survived, and went on to see in the new millennium. (Geoffrey Field)

My grandmother's house the morning after the whole street was bombed during the Second World War. The photo has a lot of personal and historical value because it helps us to remember just how devastating the war was and how much was destroyed. It will be useful to future historians because it will show them that there was a war and also what sort of weapons we had, how powerful they were and how much was destroyed. It will also show them a bit about the architecture of the twentieth century. (Nicola Doubleday, Ashford School, **Secondary School Winner**)

This photo is of my grandad when he was in the army, forty-seven years ago, at the age of eighteen. It was taken in 1953 at Farnborough, Hampshire. It was taken just after the weakest men of the army were thrown out. My grandad, Robert Wood, is on the top row, left, at the end.
My grandad wanted to join the army because he wanted to travel the world. He only fired his gun once, after being in the army for three and a half years. My grandad travelled to Malaysia, Sri Lanka and South Africa. (Sarah Smith, Brownhill Primary School)

Built in 1929–30 as the *Larus*, the first diesel drifter, and unsuccessfully converted to steam in 1931, this boat was used for drift netting for herring and in the spring sailed out of Milford Haven Long Linning. During the war it was employed as a barrage balloon boat in the Thames Estuary. The crew in 1948 were T. Utting, Sugar Aldous, B. Utting, F. Blowers, A. Utting, Bob, J. Aldous, M. Margoram, J. Powley, and Richard 'Dick' Bedingfield who is my grandad. He celebrated his seventieth birthday in June 2000. (Cally Nunn, Dell Primary School)

My great-great-uncle and his family in 1913. During the First World War he was injured in a gas attack, and although he survived the initial gassing he died a year after returning home as a result of it. I chose this photo because I think that it represents the way in which so many families were affected by the deaths of the thousands of soldiers who fought in the war. The children would grow up without a father, and many other people such as his parents and the rest of the family were all bereaved. (Sarah Dunne, Cockermouth School, **Secondary School Winner**)

My grandad, when he was thirteen years old and a bugler at the beginning of the First World War. It is special to me because it forms a link with my grandad, who died well before I was born. This photo shows a comparison between life then and life now. My grandad was fairly unusual in that, although he served in both world wars, he didn't see active service in either. (Penny Wiltshire, Cockermouth School, **Secondary School Winner**)

This is a photo taken during the Second World War in 1940. This ship was a bit like the *Titanic*. It was said not to sink but it did. The ship was called HMS *Hood*. My grandmother's brother sailed in it and he was part of the lucky thirteen. They were called that because thirteen hours before the ship sunk he and twelve other men got off. The rest of the crew went down with the ship. This picture is of personal value to me because he's one of the only survivors. (Alex Carpenter, Danes Hill School, **Primary School Winner**)

This photograph is of particular significance, both historically and personally, as it was taken before my grandfather's last operational trip. It shows the crew of the Lancaster bomber standing by their aeroplane. My grandfather was the rear gunner. They are happy as they are posing for a photograph and also because they know the war is drawing to an end. However, they are also worried – even sweating – as there is the uncertainty as to whether they will survive or return. They are also thinking of their many friends who have been shot down and killed on similar operational trips. (Abigail Temple, Danes Hill School, **Primary School Winner**)

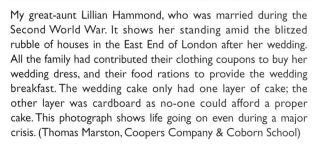

My great-aunt Lillian Hammond, who was married during the Second World War. It shows her standing amid the blitzed rubble of houses in the East End of London after her wedding. All the family had contributed their clothing coupons to buy her wedding dress, and their food rations to provide the wedding breakfast. The wedding cake only had one layer of cake; the other layer was cardboard as no-one could afford a proper cake. This photograph shows life going on even during a major crisis. (Thomas Marston, Coopers Company & Coborn School)

This picture has a significance to me because it has told me so much about my family history. The photo shows my great-great-grandad, John Joseph Purdy. He died in the First World War in France on 30 April 1917, aged twenty-three. He died before seeing his only son being born. Before he went to war he worked down the mines, which is shown by the dirty clothes and oil lantern. There is a memorial statue in Conisborough, with the names of all the people who died in the war. (Joanna Walker, Edlington School, **Secondary School Winner**)

My great-grandfather, on the right, Alexander 'Big Sandy' Stevenson, 1917. It was taken in France where he was a volunteer in the Highland Light Infantry. It does not seem special until you read the writing on the front, 'Battle of Arras, May 1917'. He fought in that battle and suffered shell shock and a crushed chest after a trench caved in on him. He was sent back to Glasgow, unfit for army duties, aged only twenty. He never recovered and became one of 2,300,000 casualties. (Lorna Gray, Duncanrig Secondary School, **Secondary School Winner**)

My grandad was in the Royal Engineers. He travelled to many countries throughout the world. During his time in the Army my grandad was stationed in Cyprus. While he was there the Greek community had a coup. The Turkish community was treated badly, causing the Turks to invade. This caused the island to be split up into Turkish and Greek areas. This invasion is historic and my grandad was there. My picture is of my grandad who was in charge of a bomb disposal team in Cyprus. My grandad was in the war in February 1972. (Stephanie Rutter, Eastway Primary School)

My grandfather Dennis Stables (left) with a friend at Melsbroek Airfield in 1944, where he served as a radar mechanic with the RAF. It shows a grandad I never knew, looking strong and young in a leather jerkin and forage cap. The aircraft pictured is an Avro Anson Mk10. NK895, powered by Cheetah XIX engines, was based at RAF Benson, making photos of the aircraft at Melsbroek rare. It was scrapped at RAF St Mawgan on 19 November 1946. Melsbroek had previously been occupied by the German Luftwaffe. It is now owned by Brussels International Airport. I would like to fly there from our local airport, Sheffield City. (James Stables, Edlington School)

This is a picture of soldiers in the First World War. As you can see they look as if they are about to have a battle. The photo was taken in 1918. In many years this photo will be of great value to many people. The photo is good for education as you can learn many things. The things you can learn are that people in the war had to work hard and also you can learn that the year 1918 didn't have coloured cameras. (Sarah Storey, Howden School)

The man in the picture is my grandad, Samuel Kenneth Johnson (born 26 May 1918 and died 25 September 1990). This photograph shows him before he fought in the Second World War. It shows the compulsory uniform. After leaving school he was an errand boy for a local grocery store in Buckley (North Wales), but he was also a member of the Territorial Army. In 1939 he had to go to Holywell Town Hall to enlist. After returning from the war he continued to live in Buckley for the rest of his life with my nanna. (Nicola Ann Johnson, Flint High School, **Secondary School Winner**)

This photo was taken of Grandma in 1941 in Japan. One day there was a fight with America, then they fought with England. But first America fought with Japan and my grandma ran into the train with her friends and she hid in the temple. When the fight was finished she went back to her house, but her house was broken and there wasn't a room. This photo was taken by her father and she is standing at the door of her house. In the future my photo will show how Japanese girls wore kimonos in those days. The photo reminds me of the war. (Kyoko Takebe, Highfield School, **Primary School Winner**)

The picture shows an anti-aircraft gun from the Second World War. It was taken when I was on my holiday in Weymouth. The picture is of special interest to me and my family. During the war my great-grandad was serving on HMS *Ramillies* on 6 June 1944. The ship was on escort duty to the biggest invasion force ever seen, D-Day. Weymouth harbour was one of the biggest ports for the gathering of the D-Day ships and men. (Natalie Jane Sutherland, Gorse Covert Primary School)

From fifteen years old my grandad worked on the farm. He left the farm at nineteen and then he got called up by the army. He spent six months at Aldershot. He started to learn to drive the big trucks and he passed his driving test. Six months later he went to Aden, and he was there for a year. My grandad made lots of friends in the army. He spent the last six months of the two years back at the base at Aldershot, and never went to war. My grandad, the one on the right, is with three of his army mates beside the big army truck. (Emma Scott, Hylton Redhouse Comprehensive)

I chose this photo because it shows the first time I can remember my dad going away for any length of time. I was five. The Royal Navy was sent to the West Indies to aid the American coastguards in the war against drug trafficking. While on tour HMS *Active* recorded a drugs haul to the value of £85 million. Sadly HMS *Active*, a Type 21 frigate, has gone. I think the future will have very few navies with people on board as computers will do the work. (Sam Pearce, Ivybridge Community College)

The photograph is of personal value as it has my dad on the right-hand side, sixteen years before I was born. I was born on Remembrance Sunday 1991. The photograph is about Remembrance Sunday, a day we remember those who gave their lives during the wars. Dad was selling poppies on Linthorpe Road, Middlesbrough. This is of historic value because of the location, landmark buildings and the insight of life in 1975 offered. For these reasons, this photograph will be of interest to future generations. (Nicola Hannah Mitchell, Kader Primary School)

Here I find the grave of my great-grandfather, H. Sandercock, Pte 14th Bn Worcestershire Regiment, on a school visit to Flanders in June 2000. I was following details extracted from the Commonwealth War Graves Commission website, and discovered that my great-grandfather, who died on Tuesday 11 November 1917 (a year to the day before the armistice was signed), is commemorated at Poelcapelle Cemetery, 10 km north-east of Ypres, grave plot XLII.C.7. (Stuart Pinkawa, King Arthur's Community College)

This photo shows my grandmother, pictured in the front row, first right, with five other women. Taken during the Second World War, it highlights the hard work and effort made by women during these difficult years. The women's workforce in the mining and steel industry significantly increased in 1939–45, as their male counterparts were enlisted in fighting for their country and the jobs were high priority. My gran had worked at the Wellesley Colliery since leaving school at fifteen. She remained there until the early 1940s, when she progressed to the munitions factory De La Rue in Lesley, where she remained until the end of the war. (Alix Thomson, Kirkland High School)

This family photograph was taken about sixty years ago. It shows my Nanny, the girl in the white dress, her sister and parents. The boys were evacuees from Gateshead. In the war they lived with Nanny at Filixkirk, near Thirsk, for four years. This photo is special to my family because it has Nanny and Nanny's family on. The boys were called Trevor, Harry and Ian. Nanny and Auntie Dot met Trevor a few years ago. I think it will be of interest in the future because it showed what happened to children from towns in the war. (Kirsty Roe, Kirkby Moorside CP)

Just after the war ended my grandad was in the RAF. He used to fly bombers and he really enjoyed it. The uniform looked different to clothes that we wear. You had to wear a green suit, a green belt, a green hat with an air force badge on it, and black shoes and glasses if you needed them. When they used to write letters to their mothers and fathers they had to use a special pen with ink. My grandad is the one on the right bottom corner. My grandad is eighteen years old in this picture. (Ebony Shewc, Lingdale Primary School)

Gertrude Allison standing with her oldest son, Ralph, and her youngest, Drummond. Seated are her sons Phillip and Douglas, in his RAF uniform with his dog. Her sons were the second cousins of my grandfather. The photo was taken between 1937 and 1939, and both Douglas and Drummond were killed in the war. It also shows the way many families were headed by the mother which changed after the Second World War. It will be of interest to future generations as it shows the young poet, Drummond Allison, who was killed in action in Southern Italy. (Owen Anthony Kemp, Lawrence Sheriff School)

This photograph of my dad was taken on 14 March 1991. It was taken during the Gulf War in Kuwait. He was in the army and this shows him standing on a road that had been shelled. I am very proud of my dad. (Sarah Briston, Lingdale Primary School)

This is a picture of my mum's family at a boarding house in Bridlington. They had just moved to the seaside and the war had ended a few years before. The boarding house belonged to my great-grandma. The whole family had moved to the seaside from Sheffield so my great-grandad could get better air, but he died very soon after. The family had to be dressed up for the photo. (Rachael Huggins, Lytham St Anne's High School)

My photograph was taken when my Boys' Brigade company was doing an item to commemorate the VE Day celebrations in 1995, during our annual display. We learnt some things about the Second World War and what it was like to live in those years. During the war my granny was evacuated. It was fun learning about it, but I would not like to have lived during the war. (Daniel Elliott, Springhill Primary School)

Left: My grandparents at their wedding. Their marriage took place just after the Second World War had ended. My grandpa had come back from serving as a radio officer in Germany. For my grandparents and for England it was the end of one era and the start of a new life. The photograph means a lot to me and my family because it shows the happiest day of my grandparents' lives. They had very little money, but they had each other. The war was over, so they could be together. (Holly Dasidson, Lytham St Anne's High School)

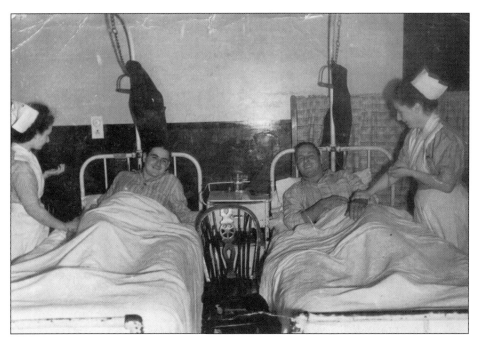

My grandad Ronald Baker and his brother Charles were tank drivers in the Second World War. They were advancing into Germany from Belgium with their regiment when they were attacked by the Germans. My grandad, great-uncle and others were injured and taken to a hospital in Belgium. The hospital was then hit by a bomb and they were airlifted back to hospitals in England. By chance my grandad and great-uncle were put in beds next to each other, and when the local papers found out they were brothers they had this photograph taken of them. (Steven Baker, Our Lady of Mount Carmel School)

This photograph was taken in the early 1970s. The lady in the picture is a distant relative of my dad. She was a northern Italian and lived on the borders of Italy and Austria. Her name was Maria, but she was known as 'Nonna' (Italian for grandma) and she lived in a small village. She and her family were poor. In the Second World War her house was occupied by German soldiers. Her husband Ricardo, named 'Nonno' (Italian for grandad) was taken hostage by the soldiers, so to protect her husband Nonna shot two German soldiers. (Joe Alexander Watson, Parrswood High School)

My great-grandad with his dog Bob in Wodston, 1916. His name was William and he was a sailor in the Royal Navy. He joined HMS *Belfast* in 1939 when it was first built. He sailed on it until it hit the mines. While HMS *Belfast* was getting repaired, he sailed on HMS *Birmingham* when it was in the Russian convoy. He then went back to HMS *Belfast*. They bombarded the French coast on D-Day and served on her until the end of the Second World War, and the boat is now on the Thames as part of a museum. (Jenna Danielle Harry, Sholing Girls School, **Secondary School Winner**)

This photo shows my great-grandmother. She was working on the land, while her husband was in the First World War. It would be a hard job for a woman because, as well as the usual chores, she would have had to do all the jobs that the men would have done. It would be just as tiring psychologically not knowing when her husband would come home. Life at home during the First World War was very tough. Growing food was important because Britain nearly starved to surrender. (Daniel Callan, Sir Harry Smith Community College)

My great-grandfather sitting on his horse (named Dolly) outside the barracks in Canterbury. He was in the VI Dragoon Guards (Carabiniers) and was later transferred to the Cavalry machine-gun corps. The photograph was taken in 1916, just before he left for the front line in France. On arriving home he was made a lance corporal and later became a corporal sergeant. It is important to me, as it is one of only two photographs of which he is the subject. He carried a large rifle in a long holster on the side of the horse and a huge sword. The horse, when being trained, had to learn how to move on its hind legs while keeping steady so that the soldier could fire his rifle with both hands. (Richard Gawith, Royal Belfast Academic Institution, **Secondary School Winner**)

My grandad, in his late twenties or early thirties, is on the left holding a gun. He was driving a Land Rover in Germany with his three mates. My grandad had to wear a uniform and a bullet-proof vest. He also had to wear dog-tags. My Mam said he was a corporal or general. This picture was taken about thirty or thirty-five years ago. My grandad had learned how to make up a machine gun. (Daniel Denning, Rodillian School)

The picture shows my great-grandfather, Major Gerald Huntbach, driving through Hanley, Stoke-on-Trent, on a victory parade. This was taken after the Second World War, although he also fought during the First World War. This picture will be of interest to future generations because it shows how times have changed and also brings back the memories of England's victory over Germany. My great-grandfather was a commander of the Tank Corps' leading H Battalion. His tank, named Hilda, was blown up during the Battle of Cambrai. This is why he is riding on the tank called Happy in the photo. (Helena Somervail, St Dominic's Priory School, **Secondary School Winner**)

My grandad in Malaya, c. 1956. He has all of his equipment on just before going off on his daily hop. He would go into the jungle looking for the Japanese bandits, who went around killing the civilians and stealing their possessions. He came into conflict with some bandits and admits it was the most horrific time of his life. My grandad is now sixty-three and he still has hot sweats and nightmares. (Daniel Taylor, Ringwood Comprehensive School, **Secondary School Winner**)

The year is 1945 and the boy in the picture is me at Trafalgar Square. The pigeon on my head could symbolise the dove of peace as the war against Germany has just been won, and in the background are servicemen and servicewomen who are arriving back from the war. (Anthony Kaye)

This is a picture of my grandad's platoon that he was in during the war. I think this is part of history because he took part in the Second World War as a pilot. I don't really know which one he is, but I know he's in there somewhere. I think he was a good pilot but he was too old for me to see him fly a plane. But he was really nice to me before he died in 1992, and I think you should put this picture on the History Channel because he took part in the war. (Helen Natalie Thornhill, Stanborough School, **Secondary School Winner**)

This is a photograph of myself (on the motorcycle) and four other national servicemen in Germany in 1952. We were all nineteen years of age and doing an eighteen-month tour in that country. There was great camaraderie between us and some good fun. As there is no national service now I look at this picture with pride, and see it as a part of history! Thanks to the men of the Second World War we did not have to fight. (Alan Maughan, **ntl Entrant**)

My uncle, Col Peter James Bradford OBE was bodyguard to the King George VI and Queen Elizabeth during the Second World War. This is historically and personally important: I understand that occasions such as these are rare – when a commoner separates King and Queen. I do not know who took this photograph but I'm sure there is a copy in the Royal Archives. This photograph was taken during 1941 at Sandringham and shows my uncle seated between the King and Queen. He was Colonel-in-Chief of the Green Jacket Regiment, also shown in the photograph. (Caroline Bagias)

This photograph reminds me of the poverty most families lived through seven years after the war ended. Christmas dinner was one small chicken between seven of us. My father took the picture. Six of us lived in the two rooms in the top flat and the toilet was outside on the landing, shared by two other families. We had had electricity installed five years previously but had no bath, hot water, washing machine or refrigerator: neither had anyone else. We all made the most of what we had at that time. (John McCulloch)

It is 1920 and both their parents and their youngest brother died in the space of six weeks. Father died from an industrial accident after surviving three years on the western front. Mother died from complications after childbirth. Split up among relatives, the six children managed to stay in touch all their lives. Twenty-one of their twenty-two children survive, and wrote these children's history so that their struggles to give their children a better life will not be forgotten. (Pamela Johnson)

In 1946, after five years as a prisoner of the Japanese, Sid Kerrison was brought home. What he suffered during that time has often dominated his life and those of his family. In 1998 his grandson James visited Japan, a conciliatory trip made possible only by Sid's captivity. In June 2000 James' younger brother Richard married his Japanese sweetheart, Yukiko, a union embraced by Sid, whose love for his grandsons has generated wisdom and courage beneficial to all concerned, not least himself. With the example and encouragement of people like Sid, the future transcends the past. (Janis Daniels)

This is one of our wedding photos, taken in September 1947. We met for the first time at the bonfire on VE night. We were both in the St John Ambulance Brigade. The guard of honour are St John cadets and are holding first aid splints. My wife has a wartime hairstyle and her wedding dress is made from (war surplus) parachute silk, for which you did not need clothing coupons. My hand is on the pocket that contains the key to our house. Homes were hard to find after five years' wartime bombing and no private house building in the war years. (Cyril Weston)

Mortlake Bus Garage, 1940. My grandmother, who was a bus conductress during the war, signing the papers for the London Transport Spitfire Fund. She was then Margaret Mary Doyle, soon to become Morris. She is shown here with bus driver Lou Hicks. This was a time when everyone was doing their bit for the war effort. (Daniel Churchman, **Sky Digital Winner**)

I am the baby in the photograph. This was the last holiday before the Second World War, at Whitley Bay – a favourite beach resort for the north-east of England. It marked the end of happy seaside holidays for the next six years. (Anne Thirlaway)

This photograph shows my father Frederick Clarke (who is on the left of the picture) helping to carry a 'casualty' from a bomb damaged house in Salford. The photo was taken in about 1946 and is, in fact, an exercise being carried out by the Civil Defence. Peace had been declared in the world, but the Civil Defence continued to train men and women in rescue and recovery well into the 1950s. It was this training, along with dedication and courage, that had helped save so many lives in the Second World War. (Barry Clarke, **Winner**)

This remarkable Second World War air strike photo is of my Beaufighter rocket attack on the ancient fortress town of Zuzemberk in Yugoslavia. Steve Schonvaldt had to manoeuvre his Beaufighter into the right position; it took much skill to activate the wonderful camera in the nose of his aircraft at the very moment I fired my eight rockets. It took nerve to concentrate on taking a photograph when anti-aircraft gunfire was expected. His aircraft was also hit by empty 20mm shells falling from the four cannon that I was firing. His photo was brilliant and our attack successful.
(Steve Stevens, **Runner Up**)

In a tent on 9 June 1999 a peace deal was signed, bringing to an end NATO's first war. General Mike Jackson (at the right end of the table) signs on behalf of NATO. The Serbs/Yugoslavs were represented by Vujovic and General Marjanovic. (Graham Spark)

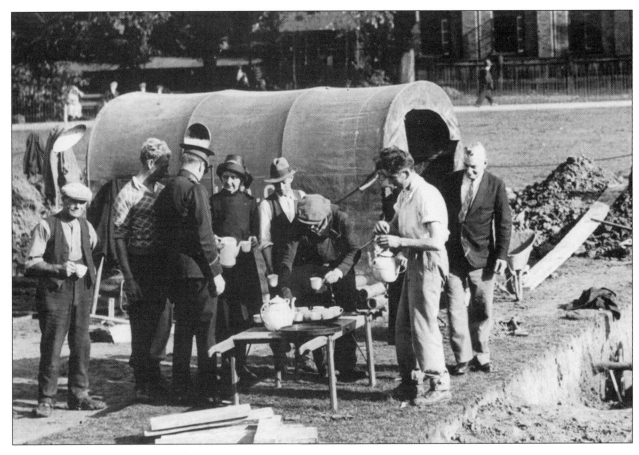

This photograph shows my grandparents, who were both in the Salvation Army and by then in their early sixties, serving tea to volunteers who were digging trenches at the outbreak of the Second World War. These trenches were intended to provide some measure of shelter and protection to people caught in air raids. Men and women, who through age or health reasons were unable to serve in the armed forces, often volunteered their services as an act of loyalty to their King and country. They should be remembered with gratitude. (Cynthia Taylor)

My grandfather died in the closing battle of the First World War. I photographed this paper so my grandchildren can have a reminder of the pain and suffering that war brings. Lest we forget. (Peter Harper)

My husband's uncle, Jack Rand, is on the far left, training with the Durham Light Infantry, 1914. He survived four years of fighting. After being injured he returned to France, where he earned the military medal in 1918 for his cool, resourceful leadership while in charge of a convoy which had to pass through a strong concentration of gas. After the war the 'land fit for heroes' did not materialise. Unemployment prompted him to emigrate to Australia to work on building the Sydney Harbour Bridge. Ironically he died in Sydney Harbour, drowned on a fishing trip, on Boxing Day 1924. (Dorothy Rand)

One of the first casualties of the Zeppelin bombing raids on London in the First World War. My grandmother, Dora Kapitko, came to this country to escape the anti-Semitic programmes in Poland in the early 1900s. She lived in the East End of London. The Germans began bombing this country in about 1916: as soon as the Zeppelins were airborne they decided to terrorise the British people, and began bombing the heavily populated areas. During a raid in 1917 my grandmother was killed – a year before I was born. It seems ironic that if she had stayed in Poland she would have died in the Holocaust. (Barney Lewis)

On 18 November 1941 this had been the High Street of a quiet Kent village, until Hitler sent his calling card in the form of two parachute mines which landed shortly after 7.00 p.m. Fifteen were killed and forty were injured, eleven of them seriously. It is believed that enemy aircraft, being chased by RAF fighters, dropped their bombs in order to escape, and Sturry just happened to be in the way. Thirty-two homes were destroyed, and not a house escaped being damaged. The lorry (JG 6353) belonged to my grandfather and great-uncle, and bears the family name. The driver has stopped for his meal during the clear-up. (Roy Gipson)

'I was among them this morning, you would not know they were Germans.' So wrote my grandfather in 1915 upon first seeing the German prisoners in his care. He is the rear stretcher-bearer on this Royal Army Medical Corps photo. Maybe my grandfather expected the dreaded Hun to have horns! Relationships developed: one German patient made and sold rings from the lead paper out of 'tab' packets. I still have my grandfather's ring, which cost him 1s 2d. (Dorothy Rand)

Peace at last – 8 May 1945. A street party to celebrate the end of the war in Europe with the young lads dressed as girls, with me in the foreground – anything for fun! Fifty-five years on the lads are pensioners and the adults dead, bar one or two. The party symbolised the end of five years of blackouts, nights in shelters and rationing. There was joy at the release from petty restrictions, and the return to seaside holidays, street lamps and the freedom to go out at night – a return to normality. (John Bailey-Smith)

My friend John Varley was in his late nineties when I took this photograph in 1971. I had read in a paper that he was the last known British survivor of the Battle of Omdurman (Sudan, 1898). Intrigued, I knocked on doors in Pimlico until I found him. We used to sit drinking Black and White whisky and smoking cigars as he told me of his long life – particularly the famous Charge of the 21st Lancers (see the plaque behind him), in which both he and Winston Churchill had taken part. (Robert Mitchell)

This photo shows the peaceful side of wartime. Although people had to endure rationing and the industrial centres of the Black Country suffered from frequent air raids, people still tried to live a normal life. This holiday photo shows the women of the family, who took the children on holiday in the summer when longer daylight hours meant fewer air raids. The men would be in the forces or working in factories. In both war and peacetime the bucket and spade was a must. (Kenneth Reynolds)

Right: When the Second World War was declared on 3 September 1939 there was no official record. My father Thomas Moore and his elder brother Joe were working for a photographic company in Fleet Street, London. This picture was taken on Victoria Embankment: see the trains in the background and the ringed lines around the trees for blackout. Although dad was only fourteen, he looked very smart in his collar and tie. Sadly he died in April this year. I know he was very proud of this photo. (Tina Edmonds, **Sky Digital Winner**)

King George VI opened the chapel at the Royal Military Academy, Sandhurst, in 1937. My father Jack Beech, aged twelve, is the third from the left of the army cadets on parade. Little did they know that in a few years these boys would be defenders of their nation. My father became a boy soldier at fourteen and served in the Grenadier Guards. At the end of the Second World War he was a tank driver in Belgium and Germany, and experienced sadness at the loss of his colleagues when his tank was blown up. (Andy Beech)

My mother's boarding house was known for welcoming Jewish refugees during the war. A new intake from Austria described their escape. Told by the Resistance they would be moving out that night, dressed like factory workers they walked towards the factory. They had to cross a bridge guarded by Germans – if stopped, they would say they were going to work. All was going well until two Jewish women, each with a yellow star on her back, were seen ahead scrubbing the paving stones. Taken aback, there was a change in their footsteps, but the Resistance whispered to them to keep moving. They reached the lorries behind the factory and were hauled aboard. One young woman looked up and said 'One of those women on the bridge was my mother.' In my mother's house we looked at her, stunned – then in a group we clung to each other and wept. (Alice Jane Campbell)

Our father, Gordon Vernon Lyall, when he was at Leeds Grammar School in 1946 – seen here with Field Marshal Montgomery. The man who protected the past generations helps my father, who went on to teach the next generation to understand that even if your back is against the wall, at least you are still looking forward. (Christopher Lyall)

Remembering VE Day with mother, 1995. It was only that day that my mother told us that she hated this room: she'd seen too much of it during the Blitz as it was their 'refuge room', complete with Morrison shelter and sand-bagged windows. This memory will be of interest (and perhaps even the cause of wonder) because it will show that, fifty years on, VE Day was still important. (Paul Windley)

This image was taken in about 1940 and shows two Land Girls. The one on the left is my aunt. With an increasing number of men being recruited into the services, agricultural needs were filled by women who joined the Women's Land Army, and worked on farms all over the country doing all the jobs previously carried out by men. (Trevor Smithers)

Two years after the war Britain is still in the grip of austerity, but at sixteen I find myself on one of the first school trips to Europe. We have passed through Calais, harbour still full of sunken ships, on to Paris, where there are severe food shortages and black bread tasting like coal, then by slow wooden-seated train into a land of plenty, Switzerland. The Swiss welcome us and all waitresses seem intent on feeding us. Future generations will wonder at how I am clad – town shoes, grey flannels rolled up – but we are all slim and fit, the result of a wartime diet. (Geoffrey Prestwich)

During the Second World War many Americans stationed in Britain married British girls, introducing the phrase 'GI bride'. Gwen was in the Land Army, initially at Shugborough Hall, then Stafford Park, where flower beds were converted to vegetable plots. It was here she met Harry, an American stationed nearby. She had to attend an interview to gain permission from the US Army before the marriage could take place. Harry was posted back to America shortly after the wedding, but Gwen had to wait until April 1946 before she, and many other GI brides, sailed to America on the *Queen Mary*. (Beverley Reynolds)

In the summer of 1969 the British Army moved into the streets of Belfast in a potential combat role. This was a unique late twentieth-century event and was widely expected to be shortlived. The two local girls, seen here chatting to two young soldiers, were not to know that their own children would see the same army still on street corners thirty-one years later. (Oliver Britton, **Runner Up**)

My grandfather, Stan Sangan. In 1943 he was in the army fighting in Algeria. Also while he was fighting in Italy, he watched Mount Etna erupt. This picture shows how people from our island community contributed to the war effort. It is special to my family because we are proud of the fact that one of our relatives helped Britain to win the war. My grandfather is still alive today and will be eighty later this year. (Jo Garnier)

A young man about to take his first solo flight, training for a little-known unit of the British Army. The Glider Pilot Regiment was the smallest and shortest lived regiment in the Army. In relative terms it also had the most casualties, seeing action in Norway, North Africa, Sicily, Yugoslavia, France, Holland and Germany. Their large troop- and tank-carrying gliders spear-headed assaults into enemy-held territory. (Arthur Procter)

The photograph shows my mother as a teenager sitting with my uncle on her knee. It is 1940 just after the retreat at Dunkirk and my mother is wearing my grandfather's steel helmet with his rifle leaning against her. It should be of interest to future generations as it shows military equipment in a civilian setting, since my grandfather would be on leave in uniform. He was later invalided out of the army with a bad stomach. Dunkirk was the famous retreat across the English Channel of the British Expeditionary Force at the start of the Second World War. (Donald Graham, **Runner Up**)

My parents Nora and Alfred Williams and me aged ten. We had just been to Buckingham Palace. My father was a police inspector, and because of all his work in the war, spending many days and nights away from his family at the air raid wardens' post, he was awarded the BEM. All the men, regardless of injuries, stood in line to receive their medal from King George VI. I wasn't that old but I was filled with pride. (Norma Murphy)

My mother taking part in a theatre production at RAF Leeming in West Yorkshire. The play is called *Angels in Love*. The year is 1966 and the young man on the left was a trainee RAF pilot who, like many of the actors on the stage, was having a break from his tiring regime. The photograph shows how the Royal Air Force has moved on from the twentieth century and into the twenty-first. (James Drennan)

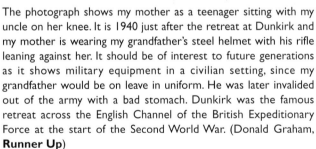

This photograph was taken in 1915, and these young people stood on the brink of a devastation and horror the world had never before borne witness to. Their fresh faces are full of an innocence that could belong to any age. As the old soldiers have all but gone this photograph maintains our links with those who gave the ultimate sacrifice. The boy standing third from the right is Private Charles L. Edwards. He was gunned down and died on the Somme on 7 July 1916, aged seventeen. It is important we never forget them. (Gary Halliwell, **Runner Up**)

Left: This is a photograph of my great-great-grandfather, Corporal Walter Clutterbuck. It was taken just before he left England during the First World War. He sailed on the *Ellengo* through the Suez Canal to Mesopotamia, where he was in charge of a 'decent group of blokes' – Arabs, Armenians, Persians, Kurds, and Indian natives. He described conditions aboard as terrible: 'the bread is full of ants and rats are running all over the ship at night.' But he kept up morale by singing to the troops on board, earning the name 'the Blackbird'. He went down with tropical illnesses, malaria, sand fly fever, cholera, and saw terrible suffering. He returned home six years later to his wife and children, half the man he was before the war. (Roberto Bernadout)

I wonder what these children thought as they stared into the camera for this photograph of their school pageant in Sunderland, *c.* 1910? Could the sailor (front left, my grandfather, William Hopper) have dreamed that during the Depression he would join the Merchant Navy as an electrical engineer, or that in 1937 he would marry Britannia (my grandmother, Norah Crosby), seated behind him? After marriage my grandfather joined other government scientists near Felixstowe, Kent, working on a new idea called radar. Early in the war the group moved away from the coast and enemy action to Malvern, Worcestershire, where my family still live. (Kate Hopper)

On the sixtieth anniversary of D-Day the Dunkirk Veterans Association gathered at Dunkirk, France, for their last combined reunion as an association. Colin Wright (of Newcastle) with a group of re-enactment soldiers followed in the footsteps of the original British troops to travel across Belgium and France sleeping in farms and trying to follow as near as possible the route to Dunkirk's beaches. A veteran after the parade through the town spots these 1940 replica soldiers and spends time catching up on his memories of sixty years before, when he was rescued from Dunkirk's beaches. (Richard Addison, **Runner Up**)

This was taken at a VE Day celebration in Haworth, Yorkshire, 2000. This picture was taken on the spur of the moment but looks as if it could have been taken in 1945, even down to the cobbled street. (Jane Robertshaw)

The VE Day celebration in Haworth again. The whole place was a total re-creation of 1945. As I asked this man to pose for me, this is the look I received – which captures the atmosphere. Everything, from shop windows to the appearance and attitudes of people made it feel like the 1940s. (Jane Robertshaw)

My grandad, Sid Gowland (kneeling down) in a German POW camp. My nan met my grandad just before he went to France. He was wounded and captured just outside Dunkirk. The only contact they had for the rest of the war was writing to each other. All letters and photographs were checked. He was not allowed to say what things were really like. I think this picture is important as it shows how photographs helped both my nan and grandad to get through the war. (Paul Gowland)

I have worked as a careworker for a charity organisation called Friend and Neighbour Service for over twelve years. During a trip to Southend I took this photo of a lady called Ellen. As the Queen Mother celebrated her hundredth birthday this year I feel all older people should be recognised, not only for their memories of two wars, but also for the difficulties they may face now, with illness, and most of all their great spirit and, at times, wonderful sense of humour. (Rosie Curran)

'Hurrah! We've won!', is the title which my grandfather, Frederick Jarvis, gave this photograph, which he took on VE Day, 1945. I was four years old. My only recollection of the war was of the victory parade in my village of Walmley, Sutton Coldfield. I went in fancy dress as Little Miss Muffet and remember my acute disappointment the following year that there was not going to be a repeat performance! To the present generation, which has known only peace in our land, this photograph captures the unbridled joy felt even by a child that the war was over. (Rosemary Longhurst, **Runner Up**)

In 1938 my family moved from London to Bognor Regis, my father believing it would be a safe place to live in the event of war. This photograph is of me in April 1939, on top of a fortified sandcastle built by three boys, who lived nearby. Looking at it now, and knowing that war was to come not long afterwards, the picture seems strangely allegorical. (Bridin Kissane)

On my first ten day leave from Ismailia, Egypt, we took the overnight train (very primitive, no glass windows, wood slat seats and we were bitten by insects) to Tel Aviv. There was a tour to Jerusalem where this photograph was taken. We saw the Dome of the Rock, the Holy Sepulchre, and the Way of the Cross. When leave finished we were unable to return to our unit as the battle of El Alamein was in progress (23 October to 5 November 1942). We were sent to Sarafand transit camp, where we had to pay 10s a day. We hitched a lift back to Jerusalem. This was a unique opportunity to explore the Holy Land. Palestine was not a state of Israel then. (Ronald Gill)

This wonderfully spontaneous moment was captured by my father (using a self-timer) in Germany in 1946. It shows a concert party striking a pose on the departure of two of its members who were being demobbed. In the centre, is comedian Stan Stennett and to the left of him my father. They were and still are the best of friends. The image serves as an important reminder of the endurance of laughter, even through troubled times, and the feeling of joy at the ceasing of war. As you can see, at the time my father titled the picture 'Happy Daze'. (Paul Pert, **Runner Up**)

A family group at Jerome's Photo Studio in Sunderland. It was taken before my grandfather went to France in the First World War, in case he did not return. He served in the Durham Light Infantry and served in India (the Khyber Pass), and had also served in the Boer War. The photo is important to the family as all of the group are no longer with us. I think it displays the anxieties and trepidation of those worrying times. The family are as follows: James and Jane Gallagher, parents; on the left my mother Betty; in the centre at the back, the eldest daughter Kitty; in front, the youngest, Jenny; and in front of grandad, James Jnr. Grandad survived the war, wounded, and had to leave the army after the war ended. James Jnr later joined the Durhams as a drummer boy. (J. Cooney)

My grandfather found this photograph during the Second World War. I think, despite being barefoot, the boy with the violin brings a ray of sunshine into their situation. It will show future generations the harsh reality, which was probably that they had walked miles, since they are on a railway track. Its historical significance is that as a lost photo of lost children it is a strong reminder of who we fought for. (Rachel Lewis)

Hartlebury, Worcestershire, was important during the war campaign and my mother, her four sisters, her two brothers and their father all worked together at Burlish Prisoner of War Camp in Stourport-on-Severn: this is where Marjorie met her husband, who was a German prisoner of war. Only one sister and two brothers still survive, as does Willy – the German prisoner, who is now a widower with three children and two grandchildren, all still living in Stourport and its surrounding villages. The photograph shows sisters and friends giving their time and labour for the war effort, but taking the enemy into their heart was a sign that love is the greatest conquerer. (Malcolm Hart)

At the end of the Second World War Europe was in turmoil. SHAPE was established mainly by Britain, the USA and France to co-ordinate the return of Europe to peacetime conditions. The picture shows two great leaders at SHAPE HQ – one civilian, Sir Winston Churchill, Prime Minister of Great Britain and one military, General Dwight D. Eisenhower, Supreme Commander – who in their different ways were key players in the liberation of Europe. Flanking the entrance on the left is a British military policeman and on the right an American. (Peter Rose, **Runner Up**)

Easter 1938: Durham County Ladies' Hockey Team tours Germany, my mother Vera playing in goal. To her dismay the Durham team was expected to join the German ladies in giving the Nazi 'Heil Hitler' salute at the beginning and end of every match. Vera organised and led the team's refusal to do so. This photo was taken just before 'bully-off' at the beginning of the match between Durham Ladies (right) and Wiesbaden Ladies (left). (Ruth Shieff, **Runner Up**)

I believe this photo is of personal and historic value as my late father-in-law was very proud to have served on the *Royal Oak*. This photo is of him with the whaling team in about 1937 or 1938. He spoke of the *Royal Oak* with great affection. (Rose Jenner)

This picture of my class was taken in 1939: we were five years old. Our innocent and peaceful childhood was about to vanish, as the Second World War had been declared. After being evacuated to Bedfordshire I went to live in Lancashire until 1945. When I returned to London everything was different, and rationing would not have enabled us to buy white outfits! I was never able to catch up with the class, and often wonder what paths they took and where they now live. (Shirley Oxenbury)

Captain James (Sam) Salt laying a wreath above the position where HMS *Sheffield* sunk (50-04S 056-56W) from the Type 42 destroyer HMS *Southampton*. The photo is of personal value to me, being a *Sheffield* survivor and also part of the ship's company of *Southampton* at the time. It reminds us all that after the guns go silent all that is left is grief. (Bob Mullen)

My grandparents Edith and Frank Massengale. My grandad was an American soldier and married my nan in August 1944 in Cheltenham. The photo was taken three weeks after my grandparents' wedding. It is the only photo of my nan in her wedding dress, which was made of parachute silk. My grandad was sent to Germany at Christmas 1944 and died in service at Hamm, Germany, in April 1945. In June 1945 my mother was born, never to have known her father. On a happier note, my nan remarried and now has twenty-one grandchildren and sixteen great-grandchildren. (Shawn Hill)

I took this photograph in 1982 while standing among the crowds of thousands who were welcoming home the very brave men of HMS *Invincible*, on their return from the Falklands War. It was an emotional day. For many of us this is the only memory of war that we have and it will never be forgotten. I hope I speak for all in saying that we are thankful we now live in peaceful times. (Sue Freeman)

The Criminal Justice Bill Rally in July 1994 was to protest at the curtailing of the right to silence, and protecting property from squatters, travellers and even ramblers. Other effects included the removal of prison officers' right to strike. It was a searing hot day, and violence erupted in front of the gates of Downing Street. Riot police on horses fragmented the march. Many arrests occurred. As the marchers dispersed into Trafalgar Square many used the fountains to cool down, and caused general mayhem. (Andrew Wood)

Coity Castle, Bridgend, near Cardiff. This was a battle re-enactment of the Siege of Coity Castle in 1404. Owain Glyndwr led the siege against Sir William Gamage to try and gain it for the Welsh but was unsuccessful. The photo is of historic value because this was the first time in 600 years that the battle was re-enacted, and on the same spot as the original battle. Future generations will see that men were prepared to give up their lives in order to regain a part of their heritage. (David Barnett)

A break between bombing missions allows time for a dedication to the girl at home. After non-stop bombing raids over Baghdad our Tornado aircraft were quickly re-armed and ready for their next launch. It was February 1991 and we were somewhere in Saudi Arabia during operation Desert Storm. I was part of an armament team whose job it was to load the most sophisticated and accurate weapons available to defeat Saddam Hussein's Iraqi war machine. I spent five months doing my 'little bit' in the most technically advanced war that the world has ever seen, and I will never forget it! (Neil Langridge)

The picture was taken hours before the ground war began in the Gulf. We had just taken part in a prayer led by the army chaplain. I had butterflies in my stomach not knowing what lay ahead of us, probably because I was so young and nervous. Future generations should know that history tends to repeat itself, especially in these peaceful times when conflicts worldwide escalate causing governments to intervene, as I found out again in Bosnia. (Nicholas Jacobs)

Poppy Day is held every year to remember the war dead, and reminds us that we must never forget the sadness that afflicts people of all nationalities living with the dreadful consequences of war. A young Japanese girl sits atop her father's shoulders. The United States Air Force estimates that on 10 March 1945 140,000 people were killed in the USAF fire raids on Tokyo, the capital of Japan. (Mike Detis, **Runner Up**)

year 2000

This is a photograph of my auntie Jackie performing in an acrobatic show at the Millennium Dome. Over the year that the Dome is open, many circus performers are able to work, in contrast to the limited number of jobs usually available to them. (Danielle Gordon Crosher)

This is me and my brother by the body zone inside the Dome. I visited the Dome on 9 April 2000. When we arrived I thought it was huge and was excited to see inside. We saw an acrobat show which I really enjoyed but I thought they were going to fall! My favourite zone was the body – I liked it when the heart was beating! The Dome is going to close at the end of the year, but I wish it wasn't as it was fun and took a long time to build. (Joanne Goldby, The Blake CE Primary School)

This photograph is of value to me because when I saw the Eye in real life I thought it was amazing that humans could make such a thing. I think it is of historical value because it was made especially for the second millennium. I think it is interesting for future generations because of its size and because it was made for the millennium celebrations. (Alex Boyd, Ashville College)

For my family one of the greatest changes in the twentieth century has been the almost universal acceptance of all humans being equal. We are a multiracial family, a type of family that was not accepted in earlier societies. Learning to live with, work with and love people who are different is not difficult unless you make it difficult. In the twentieth century relations between different people have improved, but in the year 2000 prejudice is still around, and it is now the job of all those in the new century to fight all types of prejudice. (Tara Emma Sandhu Whitburn, Clifton High School)

This is my sister in America. It took nine hours to get there by plane. Hundreds of years ago people hadn't heard of planes. The furthest my great-gran had ever been was Cardiff, only 26 miles away by horse and cart! Now we have many opportunities to travel the world and even space! In the new millennium some people travel by high-tech space rockets to Mars and the moon. My great-gran thought a horse and cart was a miracle, I think the rocket is the work of a genius, so what will my grandchildren be travelling in? (Lorna Harding, Aberdare Girls' School, **Secondary School Winner**)

I took this picture of some creative art fountains in Paris the day before the millennium. It is important to me because it gives me a memory of the last millennium. This is a place where people have a break or which people come to look at. I would say that these fountains are just as good as the ones in London.
I hope that they stay there for a long time for lots of other people to see and I hope that they will be a memory for someone else in the next millennium. (Christopher Bexter, Priory High School)

My photo was taken when the clock struck 12 when lots of people were celebrating the end of the year 1999 and the beginning of the year 2000. Lots of people went to London to see all the fireworks, but some people just stayed at home and lit sparklers and fireworks and celebrated. Lots of people will remember that day because it was the start of a new century. Our family went up to London and saw people drinking champagne and enjoying themselves. It was really great and it was really exciting and I will definitely remember it for ever. (Emma Balfour Evans, Ranelagh School)

I felt part of history on 10 June 2000 when I crossed the Millennium Bridge on the day it opened. The bridge links the south bank by the new Tate Modern art gallery to the north side by St Paul's Cathedral and can be walked across in five minutes. It is the first London bridge built for pedestrians for over a century! I hope that in the future people will always enjoy this wonderful silvery bridge for its beauty and usefulness. (Zoe Du Pille, St Catherine's School)

This is my great-great-great-great-aunt Jean in 1900. She's happy because it's a new century, can you see that? I'm looking forward to a new century too, just like great-great-great-great-aunt Jean, except it's a new millennium as well. Maybe I will live to the next century after this one. She lived at the end of Victorian times, but at the end of the next century we don't know who will be King or Queen, if there is one at all. (Catriona Graffius, St Elizabeth's RC School)

I come from Hong Kong. I came here to study. I live in the boarding house. People are really nice even though I am new. They still treat me as a friend! This makes me happy. It was a fancy dress party. People did funny impressions of important people in the last millennium. But the four girls in the photo were the most special ones. They worked as a team, celebrating the millennium directly. They trust each other and they believe that it will be a great millennium. (Lilian Hoi Kar Chiang, Talbot Heath School)

A view from the London Eye (Millennium Wheel). The photo was taken by my dad when he went on the London Eye and it looks over the Houses of Parliament, the River Thames, and many other things. In the future it will show and remind people of things that were around in the twentieth and twenty-first centuries, the things people did and places that they visited. (Hannah Eve Mitchinson, Stanborough School, **Secondary School Winner**)

This is a picture of my mum and dad's wedding. It is special because I am in it. I was very lucky to be there and I was the ring-bearer. In my grandparents' time and before, everybody had to get married. Many people in our time don't get married at all and have lots of children. I think this shows that you don't have to get married to be a happy family and that at the beginning of this millennium times have changed. Probably when I grow up things will be different again. (Alexandra Winstone-Stratos, Sutton High School)

My fiancée Pat and I went to a local Italian restaurant to celebrate the new millennium. At midnight we went outside where the owners set off a barrage of fireworks; this picture was taken as they exploded. We had already begun celebrating in style an hour earlier when the waiters were popping champagne at midnight Italian time, and this atmosphere continued with dancing around the tables until the small hours. We are getting married in August so this photo marks the start of not only the millennium but also the start of a special year for us. (Phil Chappell)

This photo, taken at the end of the twentieth century, shows part of the Thames Barrier at Greenwich, built to protect London against flooding. In the centre are the supports for the Dome which was supposed to be a sign of the bright beginning of the new millennium, but in fact has turned out to be a bit of a nightmare financially. (Geraldine Mitchell)

My sister Diane and her friends at the 1997 Labour Party Conference. They are all transsexuals and went there to campaign for equal civil rights. It is perhaps hard to accept that the men with the beards were all born girls. The photo is important because, just as the suffragettes campaigned for their rights at the turn of the last century to overcome prejudice, now it is the turn of the transsexual community to gain their equality. I feel so proud of her. (Pauline Jones)

On 1 January 2000 I wanted to take pictures of the first day of the new millennium, so I took my son out and we took some snapshots. The weather wasn't too clever, most of the country being fogbound. There has been a church on the site of St Mary's since 1190, with the one photographed there since 1810. I thought it would be good to get an important and memorable day, something that is established and a person who will be part of the future all on one picture. (Anthony Dunn, **Runner Up**)

History links the old and new: the bridge symbolises the joining of the two. I like to think of people crossing the bridge from St Paul's and making their way to the Tate Modern where future treasures may be found. The bridge was open for the first time but I could not get on it because the area was crowded with people on a Save the Children walk. As a teacher, I couldn't think of a better cause to be represented in my picture. It's an old saying but the children of today are our future. (N. James)

The West Pier in Brighton, built in 1863–6. In the middle of the 1950s it was hit by a boat and then a fire occurred, and finally, in 2000, it is being rebuilt at a cost of £14.2 million of lottery money. It has taken all this time. It was the best pier of the two, and had a ballroom; it was a great architectural structure. (Alan Bailey)

A young boy looking through the latest digital telephoto lens as he explains that he is looking forward to future technology. Joe did work experience with me and this inspired him to enter the IT field after being unsure of his future career prospects. This child realised that he had a good understanding of IT and highlighted this with his enthusiasm. (Ricky Wilson)

Right: This picture will be of interest to future generations because of the ongoing debate about the financial support the Dome is receiving. I feel this picture portrays the contrast between investment and no investment in a poor area. On the third frame of taking this subject, this unnamed gentleman appeared. When I asked him what he thought of the new addition to the area, he looked up at me and said 'what an eyesore', then carried on with his daily business. (Gary Hargerum, **Runner Up**)

I saw this man one afternoon in the busy high street of a prosperous North London borough. The streets were filled with shoppers, but no one else seemed to notice him. It was as if he had become invisible, a faceless anonymous creature who no longer mattered. If you didn't see him, then he wasn't there. This man was but one of thousands of homeless people who lived in the streets and alleys of our cities in 2000. But who was he? What was his story? For once he had been someone – someone's father, son, husband or brother. Now he was no one and I thought, there but for the grace of God.
(Bruce Paley, **Runner Up**)

This photograph was taken in Australia. It is a picture of my brother and my sister-in-law getting married on 10 February 2000. I chose this picture to show how times are changing. It is so easy and cheap to travel to the other side of the world. It also shows how the old traditional styles have not been lost: the suit and dress, and the black and white photograph. (Ben White, Coopers Company & Coborn School)

The Eiffel Tower was started in 1887 and finished in 1889. The photo was taken on 1 April 1999, 275 days before the year 2000. This picture is very special to me because 1 April is my mother's birthday; it reminds me of what a lovely day we had. We went to the top. This is valuable to future generations because the tower might not be standing for ever, so they would know what was there. (Melissa Adams, Winnersh Primary School)

An eighty-year-old bodybuilder showing his muscles at a bodybuilding competition in Southend. I have always had a respect for the elderly and I was full of admiration for his competitive spirit. We unfortunately live in an age where there is a cultural emphasis on youth. At the same time advances in medical science and improved lifestyles mean that we can all hope to live longer. I hope this photograph will serve as an example to future members of the 'Third Age' that it is never too late in life to pursue interests and have fun. (David Cross)

More and more people are ordering goods from the internet and having everything delivered to their doorstep. Pictured in this photograph taken in about 1947 is my uncle Steve Pickles, beside his and my father's mobile shop. This family business provided a much needed service to the community for thirty-five years. Then, as now, the shop with all its stock was made available on the doorstep. (Gary Pickles)

I took this photograph at our friend's New Year's Eve party, 1999. As the last few minutes of the old year ticked away, we all gathered around the television to see the familiar count down with Big Ben. As the chimes sounded the house erupted with excitement – it was at this precise moment I took this photograph. We all felt so privileged to have been able to witness a brand new millennium. (Diane Turner, **Runner Up**)

Even though John suffers from autism he displays 'normal' traits. One of these is to fixate on a task or object. While he was playing on the Gameboy he looked like any other child. It is a sign of the times that children have slowly stopped communicating and playing with others and now, like John, can only empathise with electronic boxes. (Benjamin Birchall)

I guess both the historical and personal value of this picture is when and why it was taken. Like the majority of people who are lucky enough to live on this beautiful island I suppose I was hoping for the dawning of a new beginning. Maybe next millennium. (Jim Maginnis)

The Coventry Hippodrome was built in art deco style in 1937 to the highest standards and could seat 2,200 people. Entertainers including Laurence Olivier, Norman Wisdom, Ken Dodd, the Beatles and Cliff Richard have delighted packed audiences. Pantomimes at the Hippodrome were legendary and such fun. The Hippodrome closed in 1985 and is presently used as a bingo hall.
It will shortly be demolished as part of Coventry Council's Phoenix initiative, although thousands of people signed petitions to keep it. A clock and a new entrance to the motor museum next door will soon replace the Hippodrome.
(John Osborne)

I saw this new Beetle and was amazed at its shape. It really shows how different cars have become – all streamlined and futuristic rather than the square boxes of yesteryear.
(Glenn Campbell)

After all the hype, the fears and expectations that led up to the new millennium, this photograph, which I took on Caistor Beach as the sun came up, captured for me the truth and real meaning of the moment: a special dawn with all its beauty, and the feeling of hope for the world's future.
(Jaqueline Williamson, **Runner Up**)

Winners

Overall winners

Donald Morris, Staffordshire; Glyn Picton, Berkshire; Kenneth Broomfield, North Yorkshire; Nesta Hoyle, West Yorkshire; Karen Parsons, Leicestershire.

Winners

P.K. Wengyel, Derbyshire; John Finnigan, London; Robert Plumley, Essex; Richard Martin, Devon; Katharine McKinnon, Merseyside; Dorothy Cole, Essex; Cyril Levy, Essex; Roger Aspray, Dorset; Mary Peet, Lincolnshire; Audrey Trumper, Worcestershire; Derek Harding, Gwent; Frank Gregory, Kent; Nina Iles, Middlesex; Arthur Colburn, Swansea; Rachel Boothby, Lincolnshire; Robert Broeder, Middlesex; Barry Clarke, Kent; Wendy Carlson, Bath; Dawn Pavitt, Bristol; Freda Gibbon, West Glamorgan; Lorraine Morley, London; Gillian May, Devon; John Dinham, Birmingham; Nigel Gooch, Norfolk.

Royal British Legion Winner

Michael Hawkins, Dorset.

Secondary School Individual Winners

Laura Miller, Craigholme, Glasgow; Rebecca Ryan, Ysgol Pencoed, Bridgend; Kim Stephen, Bridge of Don Academy, Aberdeen; Daniel Cox, Emma Russell, Ringwood Comprehensive School, Hampshire; Nicole Andrews, Wyggeston & Queen Elizabeth I College, Leicester; Serena Fuller, Ashford School, Kent; Jenna Harry, Sholing Girls Secondary, Hampshire; Helena Somervail, St Dominic's Priory, Staffordshire; Joanna Walker, Edlington School, Doncaster; Caroline Fletcher, Brownedge St Mary's RC, Preston; Obinna Nnajiuba, Coopers Company & Coborn School, Essex; Deborah Neale, Cockermouth School, Cumbria; Laura Keating, Andrew Pellegrini, Honor Hewett, St Paul's Catholic College, West Sussex; Laura Pinkerton, Duncanrig Secondary School, Glasgow; James McAlonan, Lytham St Annes, North West; Jemma Tivendale, The Kingswinford School, West Midlands; Lizzie Bush, Clifton High School, Bristol.

Primary School Group Winners

Hillhead Primary School, Caithness; Highfield School, Berkshire; Danes Hill School, Surrey.

Secondary School Group Winners

Ashford School, Kent; Duncanrig Secondary School, Scotland; Cockermouth School, Cumbria; Stanborough School, Hertfordshire; Ringwood Comprehensive School, Hampshire; Royal Belfast Academy, Belfast; Ackworth School, Yorkshire; Aberdare Girls School, Aberdare; St Paul's Catholic College, West Sussex; Flint High School, Flintshire.

Secondary School Group Entries

Aberdare Girls School, Aberdare; Ackworth School, West Yorkshire; Royal Belfast Academic Institution, Belfast; Ringwood Comprehensive School, Hampshire; Ashford School, Kent; Stanborough School, Hertfordshire; Cockermouth School, Cumbria; Duncanrig Secondary School, Glasgow; St Paul's Catholic College, West Sussex; Flint High School, Flintshire.

Sky Digital Winners

Daniel Churchman, Middlesex; Andrew Leese, Newcastle; Stephen Bennett, Milton Keynes; Tina Edmonds, Essex; Andrew Halling, Essex.

Runners Up

Dorothy Rand, Durham; Ken Waugh, Bath; Peter John Harper, Wolverhampton; Helen Thake, Swindon; Colin Jagger, Grimsby; Thomas Hill, Jersey; Pauline Morris, Warrington; Diane Turner, Dudley; Jaqueline Williamson, Norwich; Anthony Dunn, Cheshire; Bruce Paley, London; Rosemary Longhurst, Devon; Steve Stevens, Worthing; Oliver Britton, Potters Bar; Paul Pert, London; Donald Graham, Carlisle; Gary Halliwell, Bolton; Mike De Tisi, London; Peter Rose, Cardiff; Richard Addison, Lincolnshire; Ruth Shieff, London; Ronald Prince, Derby; Raymond Kennedy, Bristol; Jean Moore, Plymouth; Maria Estevez, Leicester; Alan Ainsworth, Glasgow; Jason Dawson, Norwich; Bill Radford, Dorset; Derek Harding, Gwent; Wendy Hobart, Gloucestershire; Pamela Hill, Lichfield; Beverley Reynolds, West Midlands; Janet Stevenson, Cheltenham; John Carroll, London; Kate Hopper, Worcestershire; Pogus Caesar, Birmingham; Cyril Kellman, Reading; Kevin Wilton, Bristol; Andrew Macleod, Edinburgh; Bernard Kat, Newcastle upon Tyne; Albert Couldwell, Sheffield; Joy Gordon, London; Ann O'Neil, Portsmouth; B. A. Cooke, Herefordshire; Nigel Gooch, Norwich; W. Johnstone, Cumbria; Gary Margerum, Kent; Robin Sharples, Lancashire; Sylvie Duncan, Bristol; Tacina Rae-Smith, Dorset.

ntl Entrants

Andy Beech, Nottinghamshire; Alan Maughan, Oxfordshire; Glyndwr Hughes, Glamorgan.